From Provence to Mekong Delta DE-SO Architects

From Provence to Mekong Delta DE-SO Architects

Texts by
Olivier Souquet & Christine Dalnoky

Edited by
Oscar Riera Ojeda

Photography by
Hervé Abbadie, Hiroki Oki
& Giuseppe De Francesco

OSCAR RIERA OJEDA
PUBLISHERS

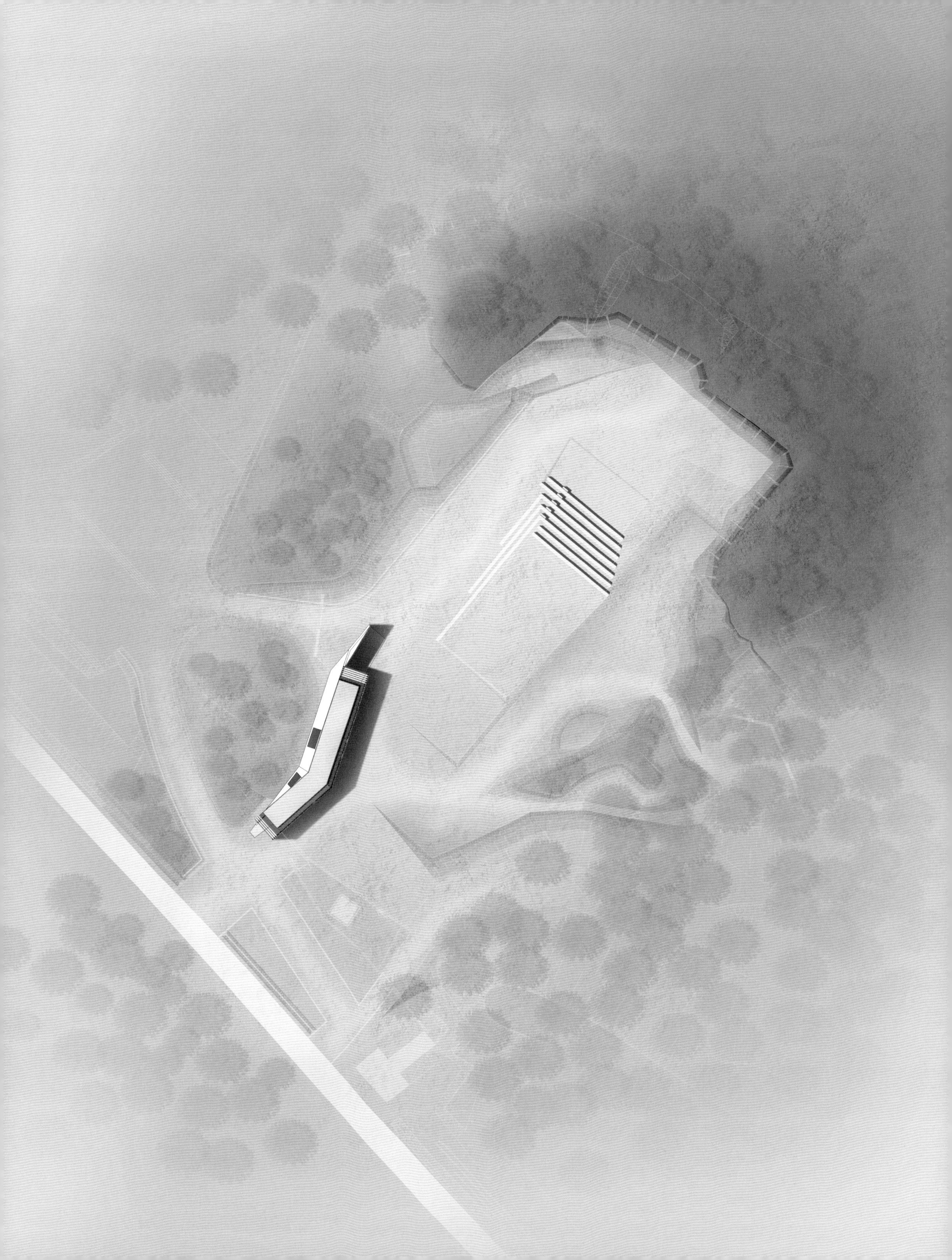

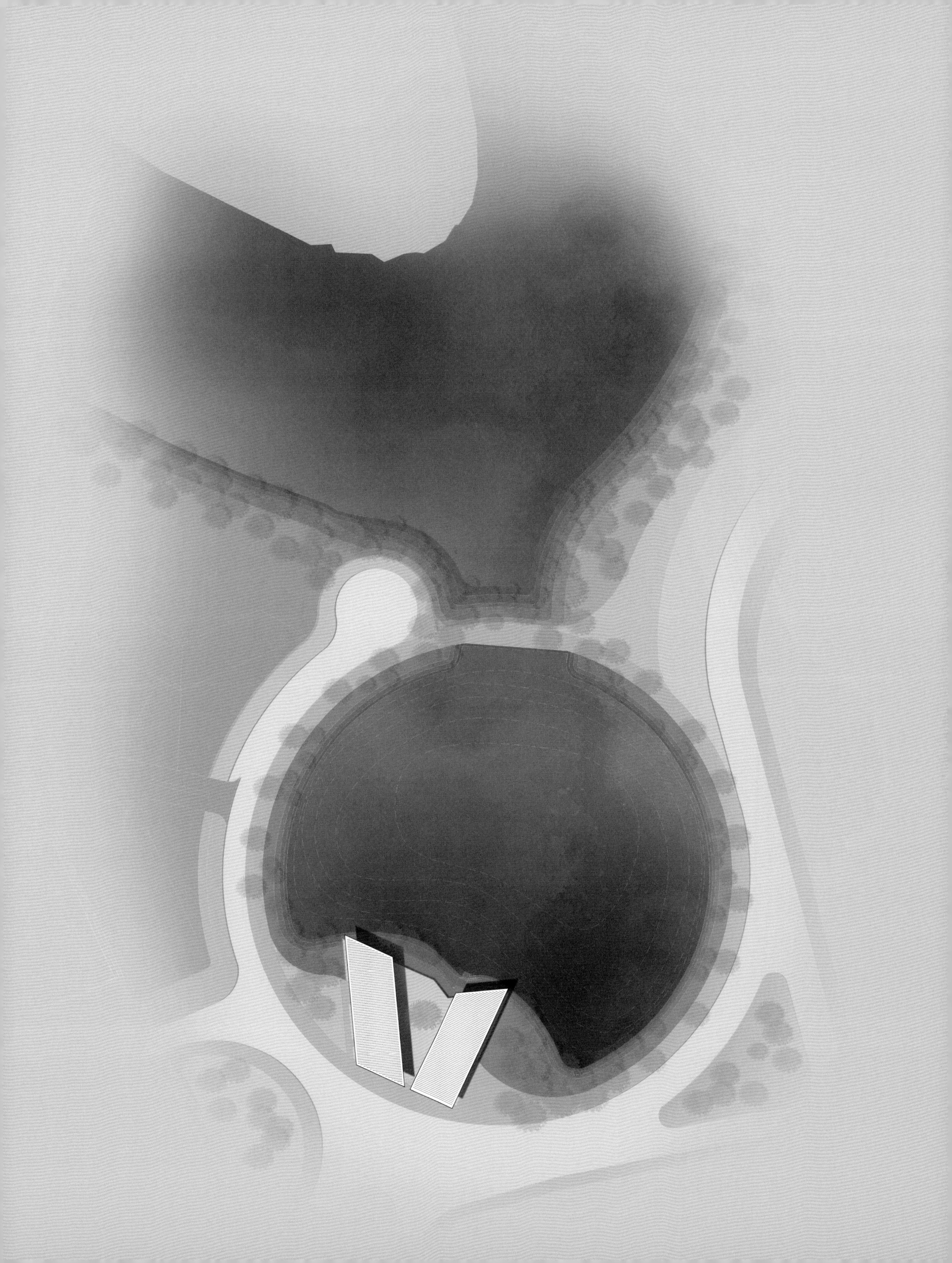

Contents

Introduction

Two climates, two continents, two buildings…

| Olivier Souquet

The visitor centers in Can Gio, south Vietnam and Bruoux en Provence in the south of France are designed by the architectural firm DE-SO and DE-SO Asia. Both buildings integrate into their respective landscape and climate. The Bruoux en Provence building was built in 2010 and Can Gio in 2020 – 10 years later.

Slightly elevated above natural ground level, the Can Gio pavilion reception areas benefit from the cool sea breeze – a naturally ventilated gazebo that overlooks the mangrove swamp.

Built into a hillside, the Bruoux en Provence mines visitor center concourse benefits from thermal inertia and the freshness of the ground, burying into the earth to create a shaded "cool" space for visitors that overlooks the ochre cliffs paved square.

Each building is built from local materials – a constructive choice that favors short supply circuits of the natural materials – laterite stone in the sandy mangroves of the Saigon River, timber and concrete from a site in Provence.

The Can Gio building is the grey color of the mangrove silt, and Bruoux the orange the color of the ocher in Provence. Both buildings express a special strong attachment with the ground.

Their abstraction and the landscape views are key to the design of these two projects. In its own way, each frames views of the natural landscape. Views that are like abstract paintings composed of colors strongly imbued with the air moisture or sunlight intensity.

At night, the moucharabiehs – clad in solid laterite stone bricks at Can Gio and in vertical pine screen at the Mines de Bruoux visitor center – create subtle, magnetic lanterns whose light changes in accordance with visitor movement within.

An angular geometry composes the layout of both projects in contrast with the flowing lines of the surrounding topography.

As since the beginning of architecture – geometry and geography intertwine to accentuate their expression.

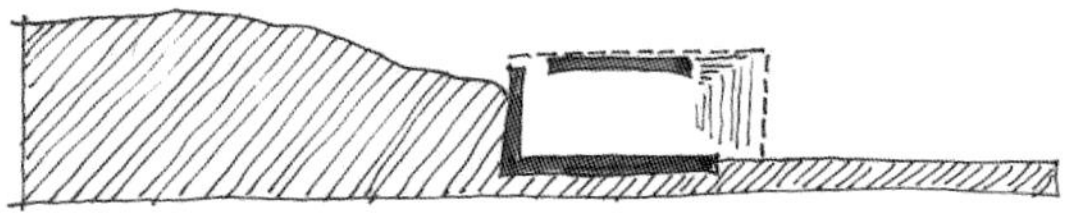

Ochre Mines of Bruoux Pavilion

Description

Project Credits

Contractor
City Of Gargas

Subject Mastery
Architects: De-So Defrain — Souquet
Mathieu Labardin (Studies)
Landscaper: Christine Dalnoky

BET TCE
Betrec (Grenoble)

BET Fuilde
Ingeflux (Orange)

OPC
Nathalie Capelli

Companies
Special works: Alteam, Axima
Structural work: Entreprise Moretti,
Green space: Provence Horizon Vert
Framework/Wood: Jean Morel et Associes
Interior joinery: Marc Angosto
Locksmith: Pierre Gregoire

Materials
Wood, site concrete

Surfaces
Usable building surface, reception: 150 m²
Length of the developed course of the mines: 250 m.
Outdoor facilities: 4 hectares

Cost
Construction cost: € 1.85 million

Program
The wooden frame comes from a local industry, the walls are in site concrete. As the site is highly constrained, a Cliff security in the Parc du Lubéron has been installed.

Sustainability Approach
Optimization energy only of the reception building.
BBC building 50 kw / m² / year.

Development of Ochre Mines into a Tourist Location, Bruoux, France

| DE-SO - François Defrain and Olivier Souquet with Christine Dalnoky

A Site, a Landscape and a Time Capsule

The city of Gargas ("mountain" in Provençal) is located in southern France and is home to the site of Bruoux where the architecture firm De-So and Christine Dalnoky's architectural and landscaping project was built.

The purpose of the project was development of ochre mines into an organized tour including an open air amphitheater for art festivals. The site is predominantly made up of a natural mineral: ochre, pure clay (kaolinite) combined with ferric rock (iron hydroxide) and used as a coloring pigment since prehistory. The rock makes this region a unique "Provençal Colorado" recognized as a biosphere reserve by UNESCO. It also has a biotope area for rare plants.

It is an unusual location whose unique brightness is due to the colors of the rocks – yellow (goethite), brown (limonite) and red (hematite) – as well as the esthetic power generated by the work of 19th century miners. Looking further back in history, an ancestral past is unearthed, including prehistoric ochre murals. The bedrock of the architectural and landscaping project delivered in January 2009 was built on a plot of land steeped in and shaped by the different historic eras.

The making, shaping and image of the location were not dictated by any intention. It traces back to a mining past and the requirements of exploitation as well as the region's complex and rich geography and climate.

This raw, wild and perennial look was painstakingly preserved by the combined intentions of the architect and landscapist as a tribute to the Past and Nature.

Staging Nature and Vegetation

Choosing the right way to stage the site in its natural landscape is one of the important features behind the project's success, whose focus was the relationship between the natural site and mining.

The mine is a multi-cavity (galleries) imprint in nature. The cliff was hollowed out in the 19th century for international exploitation.

In the 2009 development project, only the exterior soil was worked on without bringing in external materials. The architect and landscapist respected nature by working with the local elements of the site, and with an eye for environmental issues and sustainable development.

As the construction proceeded, it was essential to respect the natural topography of the site as well as its ecosystem.

The landscaping work that was performed leveraged the existing resources of the ochre landscape. The distinctive characteristic of the ground is that it is a barren and sandy ground unfavorable to lush nature.

In order to enable the forest ecosystem to regenerate and shade certain strategic spots of the walking tour, it was necessary to move a few trees and plant new ones. The replanting process respected the biotope and was focused toward pine trees as well as evergreen and white oaks, specifically:

– along the road of Croagnes and on the platform of the parking lot where no vegetation grew.
– on the promenade of the mine where the amphitheater sits;
– all along the path connecting the exit of the mine tour with the reception building.
– to patch up the reshaped embankments in order to accommodate passage.

The Traces of the Past: The Miners' Work

Today, Gargas is still one of the last few villages in Europe where ochre is still exploited. The transformation of Bruoux's mines into an organized tour is designed in an effort to enhance a mining heritage bound up with the present. The tremendous heights and depths of the galleries – over 6 meters (19 feet) high – are testimony of the hard toil performed by men.

Scale

On visuals and maps, the architect and landscapist decided not to feature any construction, character, dimension, etc. which may give a sense of the scale and height of the site. The objective was to recreate the authenticity of the ochre cliffs by sustaining a surprise and discovery effect when first arriving at the site.

The Locations

The entrance of the site:

Stepping inside the site one gets a view of the entire ochre cliff. The development was designed in such a way that the visitor's eye can capture a whole range of elements, colors and materials, an immersion intended by the designers. To achieve that effect, the designers built the reception building (ticker booths, cafeteria, etc.) by shifting it leftward to avoid screening the view of the cliff. A power substation in the immediate field of vision, at man size level, and at the entrance of the site, was concealed by a brown wire mesh in order to blend in with the surrounding natural range of colors. The substation was shut in with ochre concrete low walls from the site, thus avoiding importation – a highly environment-friendly commitment.

The promenade (Esplanade) facing the mines:

Miners carved away at the outside walls of the cliffs and were thus able to clear platforms outside the gallery entrances. It is a large slope that sweeps down to the foot of the cliff. The architect and landscapist capitalized on these carvings by building an "amphitheater promenade" including stair-like layered tiers to accommodate art festivals. The spectators will attend the various shows against a unique stage backdrop: the ochre cliff with the mine entrances.

Visiting the Mines

Access:

A 30 minute walking tour, uninterrupted, stretching across 650-meter (2130-foot) galleries, was developed. The journey weaves its way through several galleries of various heights ranging from 3 to 6 meters. Two gates built from carved wood were designed as light and air filters and lead to the entrance and exit of the mines. Various gallery entrances made by miners on the façade of the cliffs were shut off to harmonize and secure the site, using Corten steel doors which will take on an orange-brown color as they age and tone in with the color range of the site.

Inside:

Like the outside developments the inside developments of the mines were also simple, pared-down and free of any pervasive detail effects. Only the distinctive spatial qualities of the location and its history were highlighted by two types of lighting:

– walkway lighting was installed on the ground throughout the walking tour using LEDs.

– this background lighting was complemented with accent lighting to set off the remarkable spaces. Intense light sources were set up to complete it.

A Reception Building that Blends with the Site

Second step in the program: its position on the site keeps away prevailing west winds. The building is a covered walkway made from carved wood which filters out the rays of sunrise. The main façade, which looks onto the promenade where the amphitheater sits, is also made from carved wood, serving as a natural filter echoing the vertical rhythm of the existing tree trunks. It sits on the edge of a small woody hill thus making for a new horizon line. This dynamic broken line steers the gaze towards the cliffs.

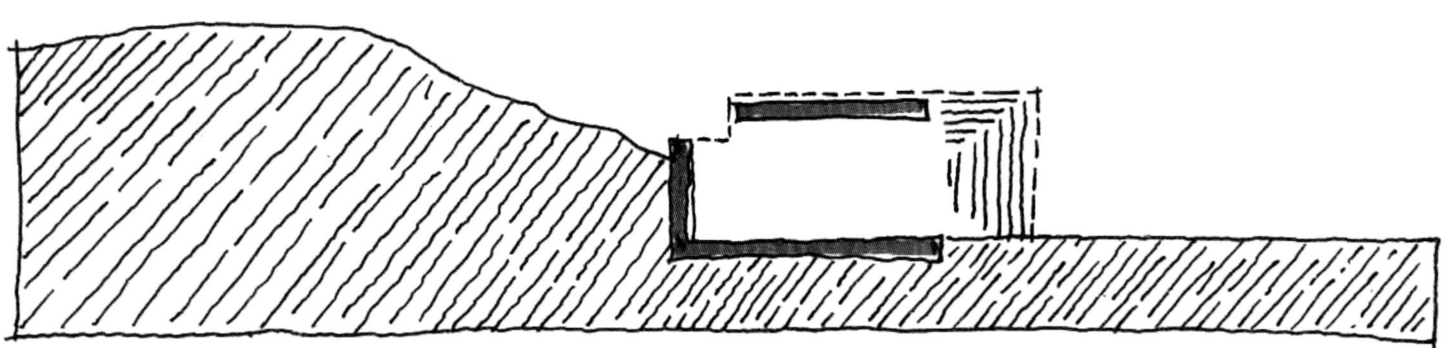

Wood as Natural Material and Filtering Skin of the Building

The reception building was designed as a covered courtyard. It houses under a wooden mesh with a single covered gallery: the front desk, ticket booth, shop, restrooms and the cafeteria which has a terrace giving a panoramic view of the ochre cliffs. Also, the bar has a storeroom for preparing hot drinks after visiting the mines where temperatures are quite low.

The wooden courtyard, through the transparency of its filter wall (wooden and glass interior façades), opens out onto the clearing located at the end of the walking tour and the shade garden protecting against the warming sunrise and the south. The soffit of the building is nail-down flooring, without suspended ceiling and visible from the road.

An Environment-Friendly Building

An ochre light-colored concrete retaining wall built on the hillside makes up an "amenity-based" layer comprising the exterior patios. Those patios give a natural indirect light inside the building. The building has a vegetated roof to:

- achieve a harmonious match and integration of the construction in the natural environment.
- obtain superior thermal inertia of the overall system by providing a climatic amenity area.
- ventilate the building simply and manually (the restrooms are water-tight but not air-tight and do not require maintenance and use).
- use waste water from the vegetated roof and return the runoffs to the site.

Drawings

Masterplan

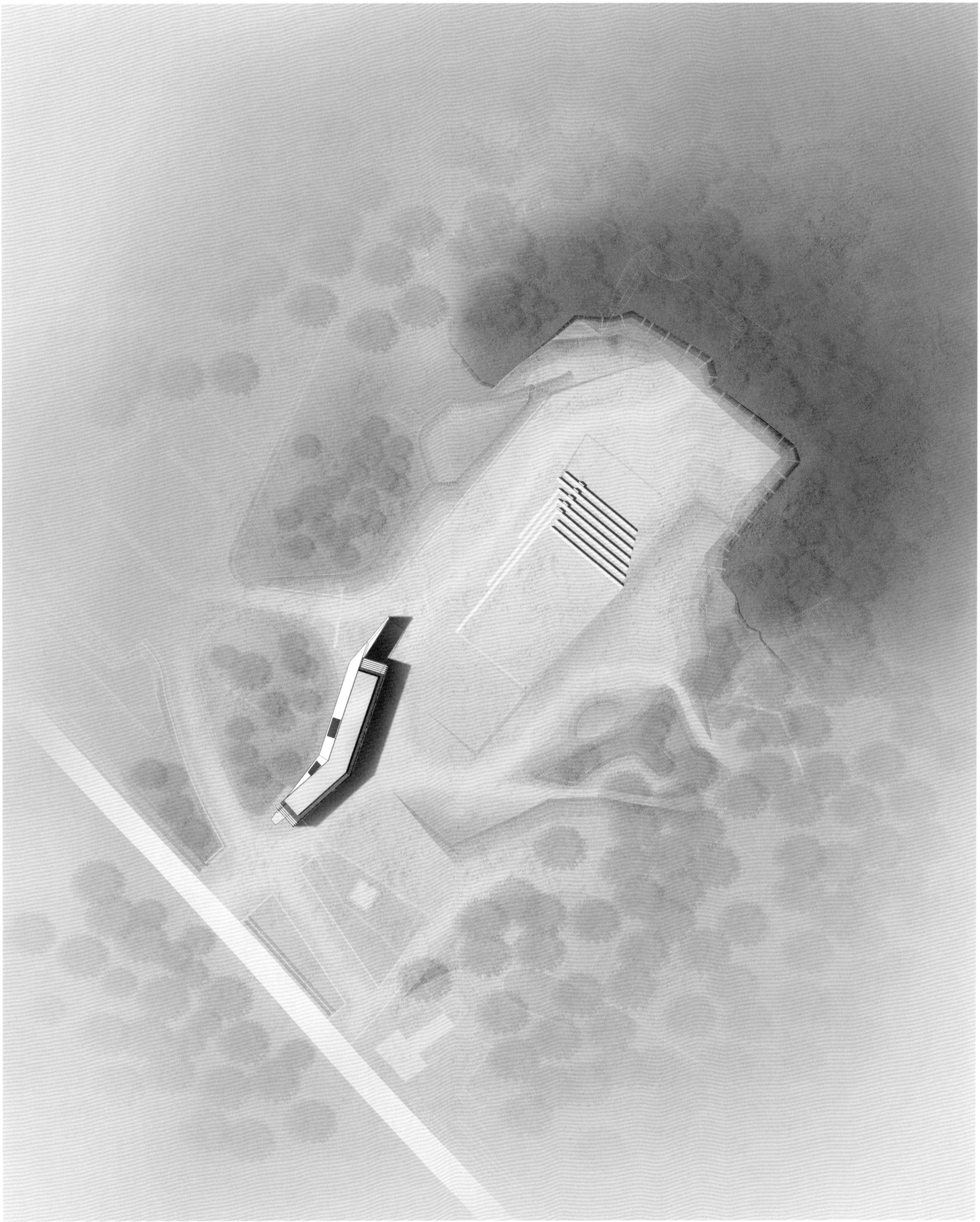

entrée de
la mine
théâtre
jardin d'ombre
esplanade
parking
entrée

clairière
zone fraîche
sortie
la mine

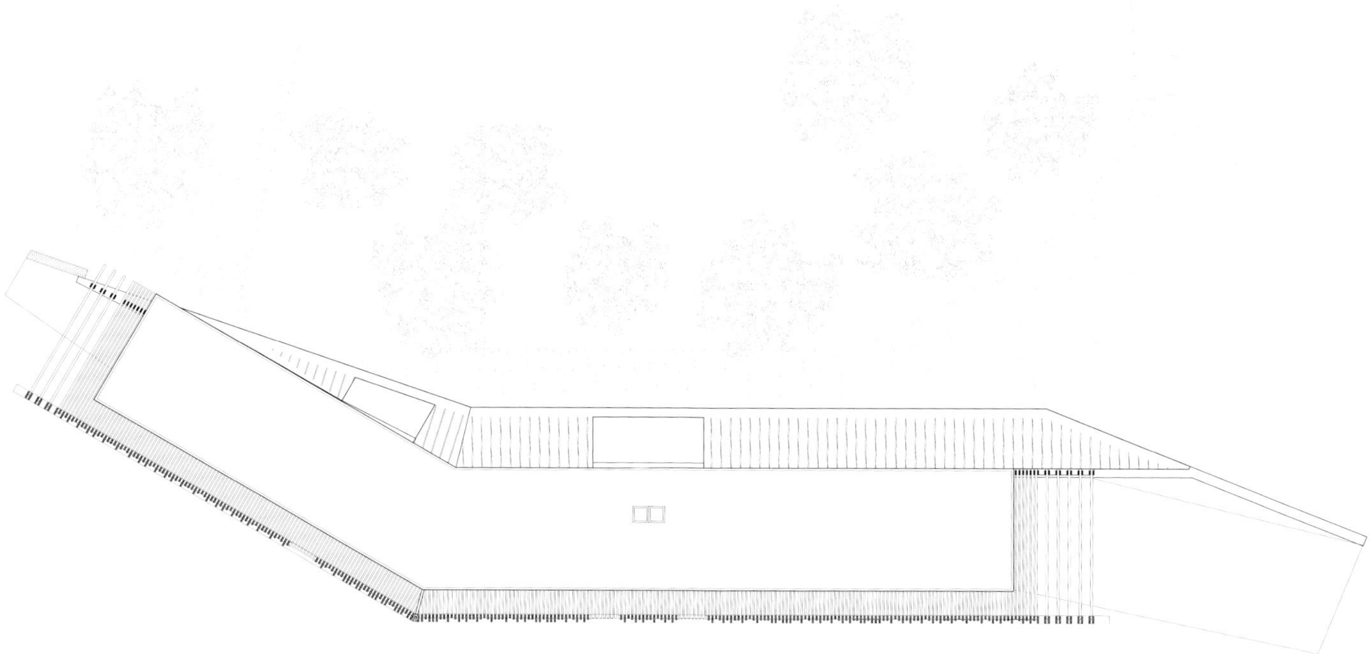

Roof plan

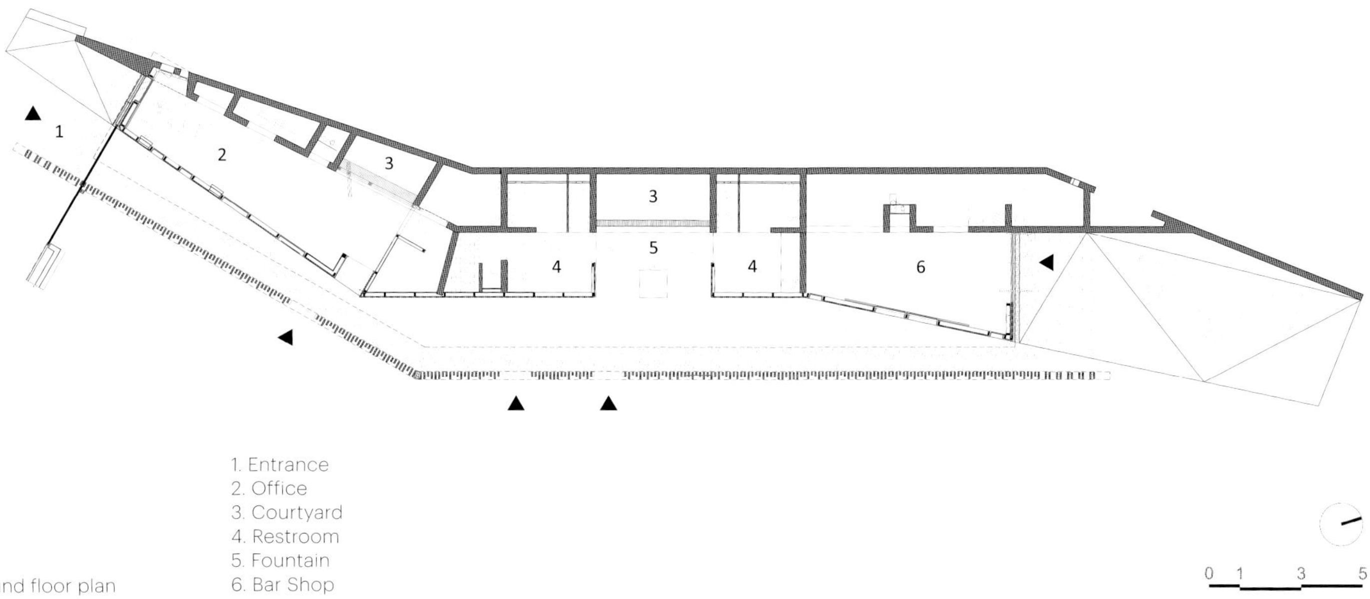

1. Entrance
2. Office
3. Courtyard
4. Restroom
5. Fountain
6. Bar Shop

Ground floor plan

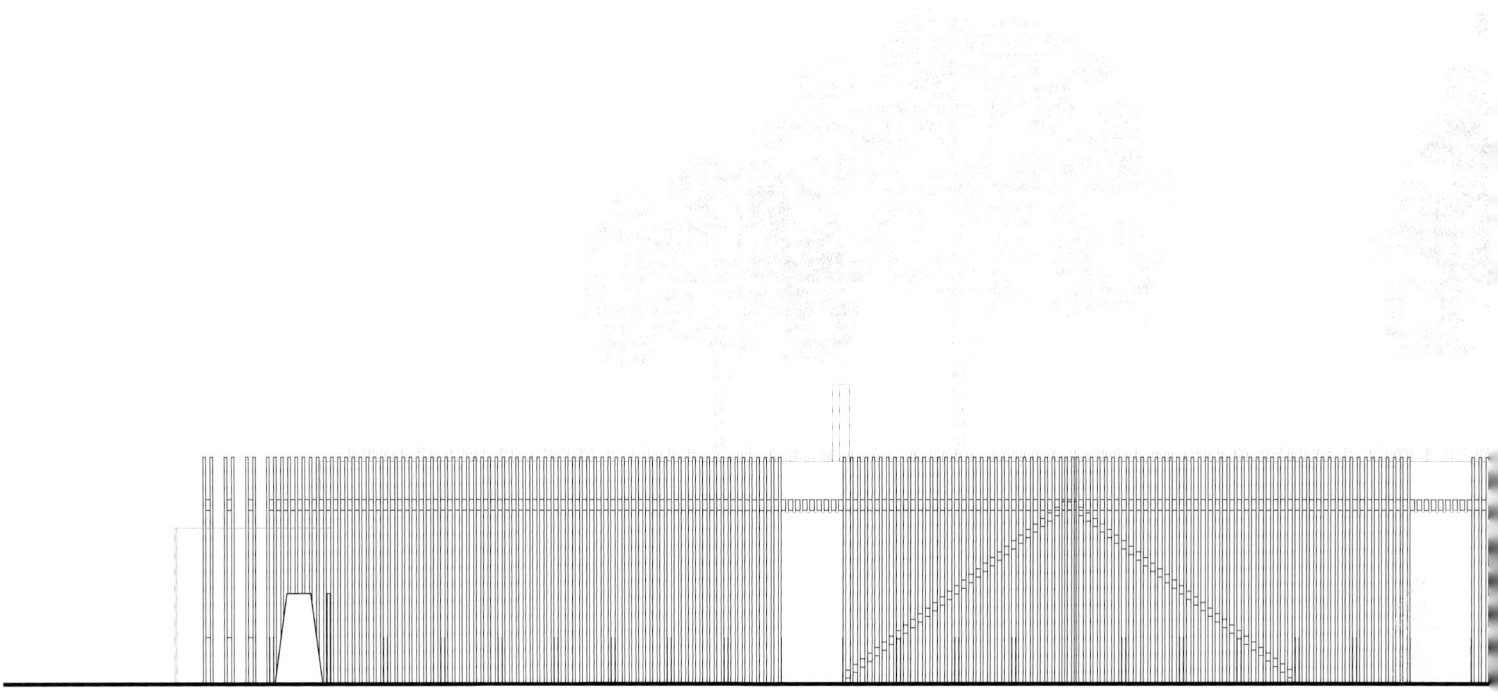

Elevation

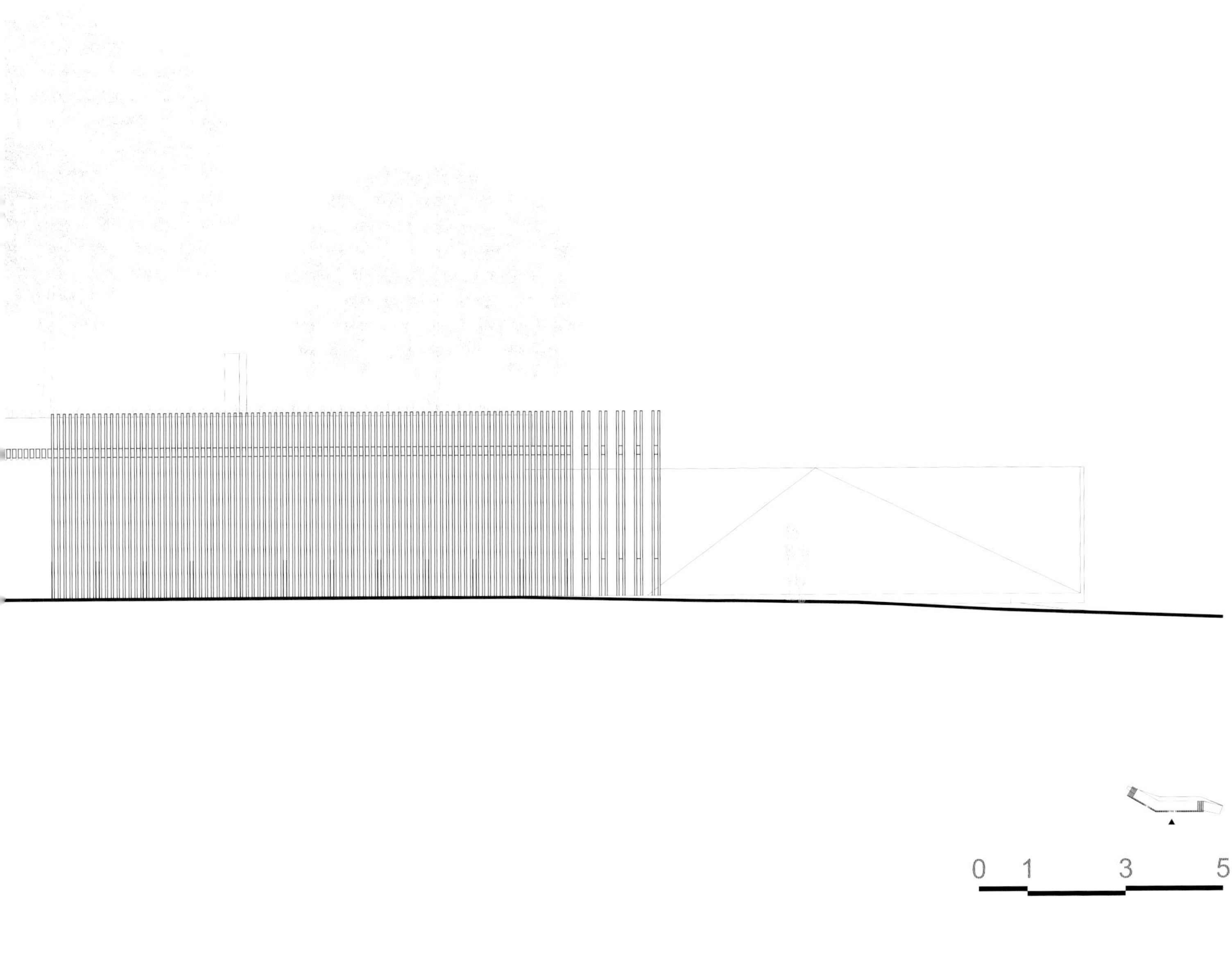
0 1 3 5

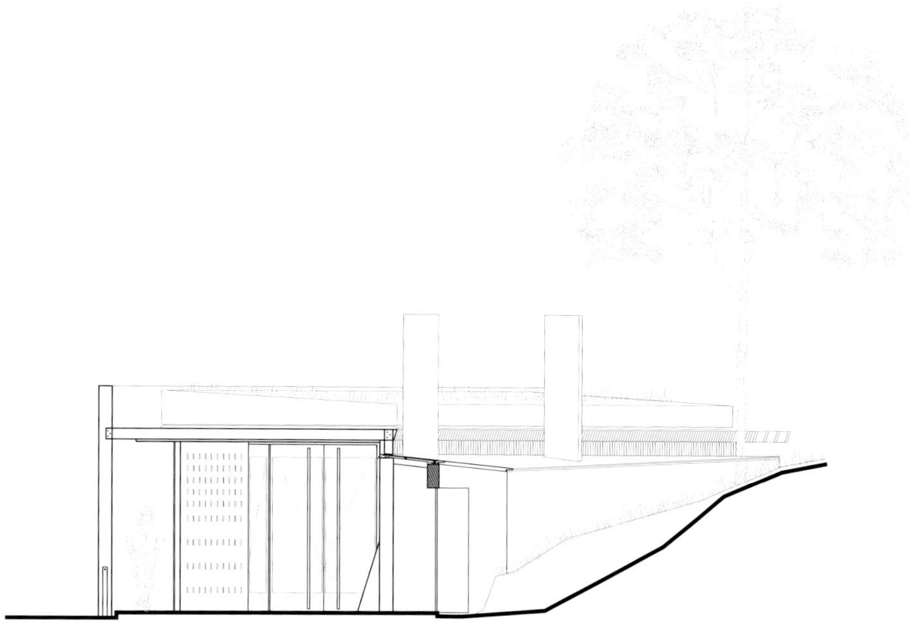

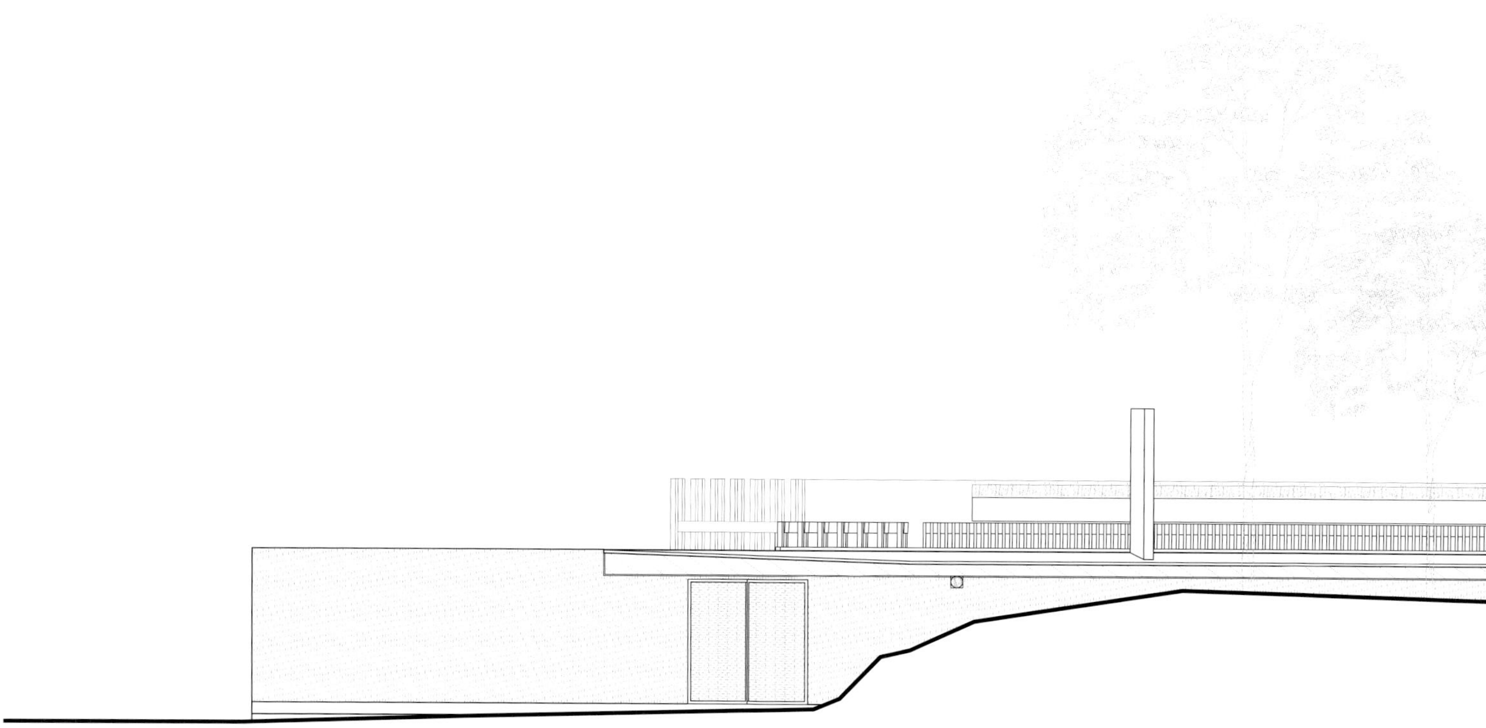

Elevations

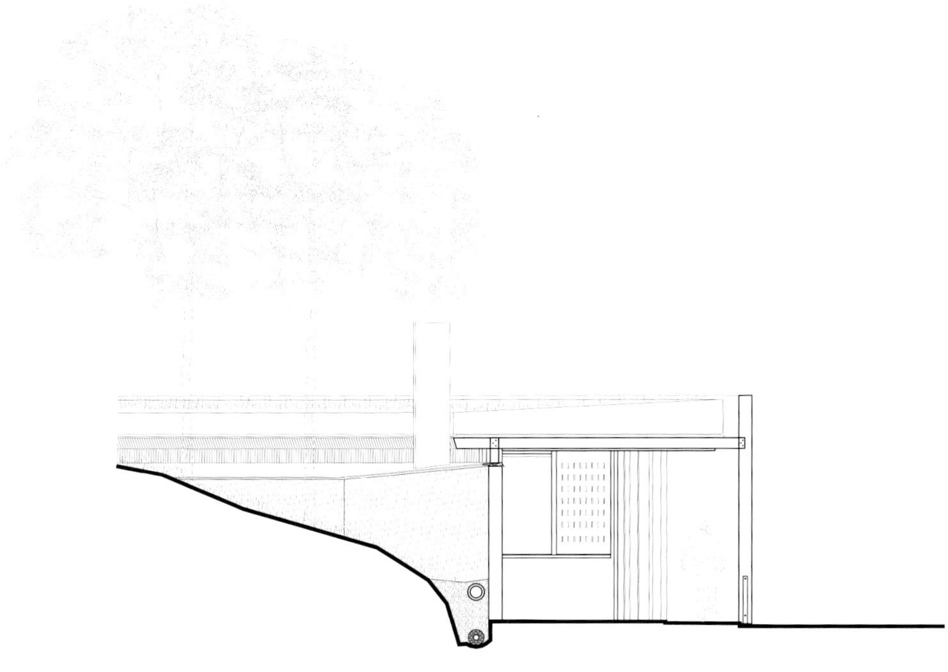

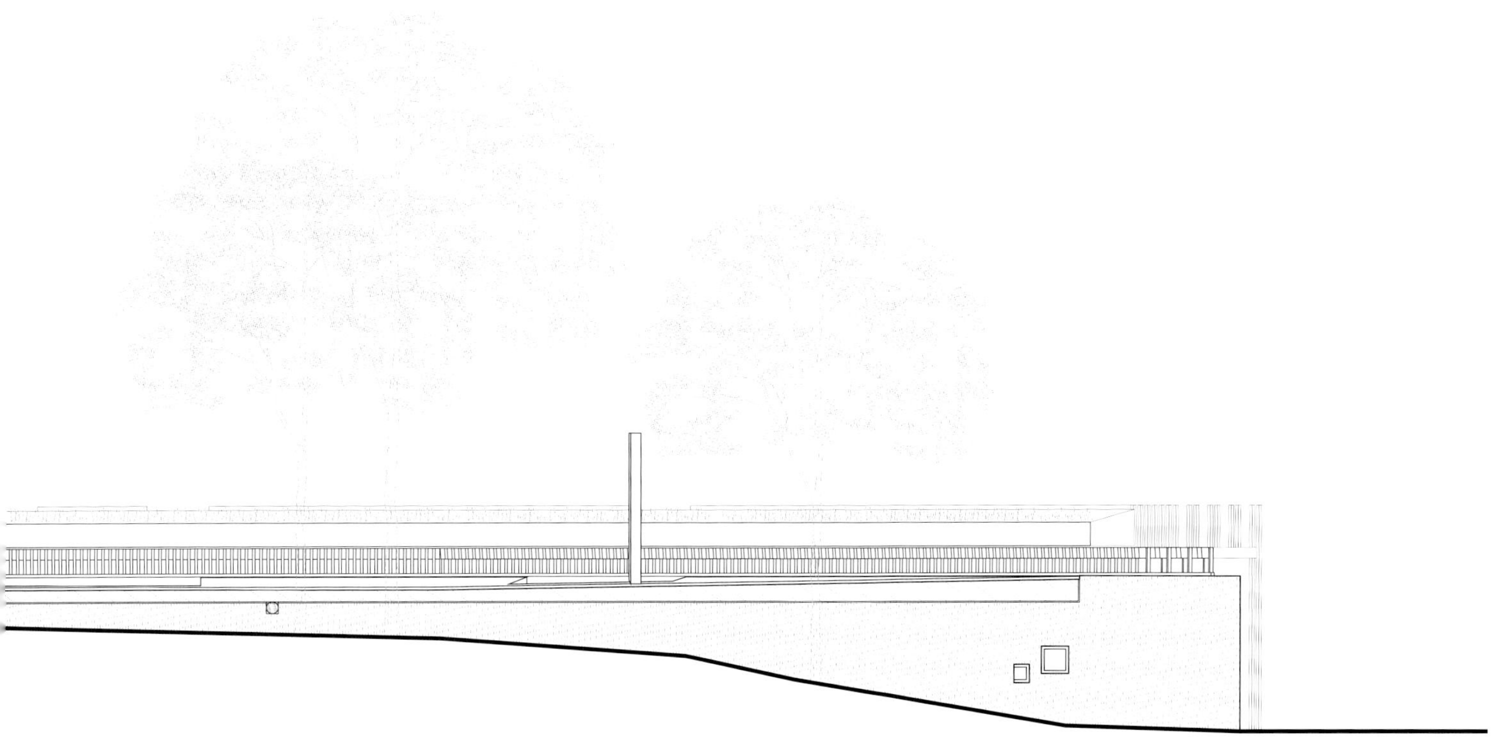

0 1 3 5

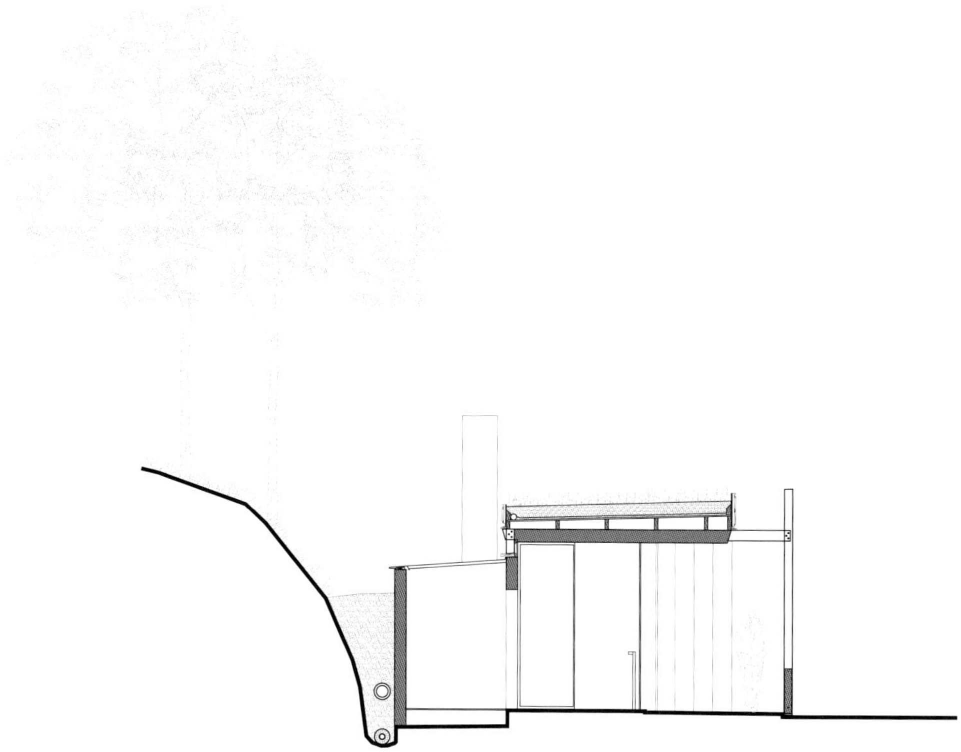

Sections

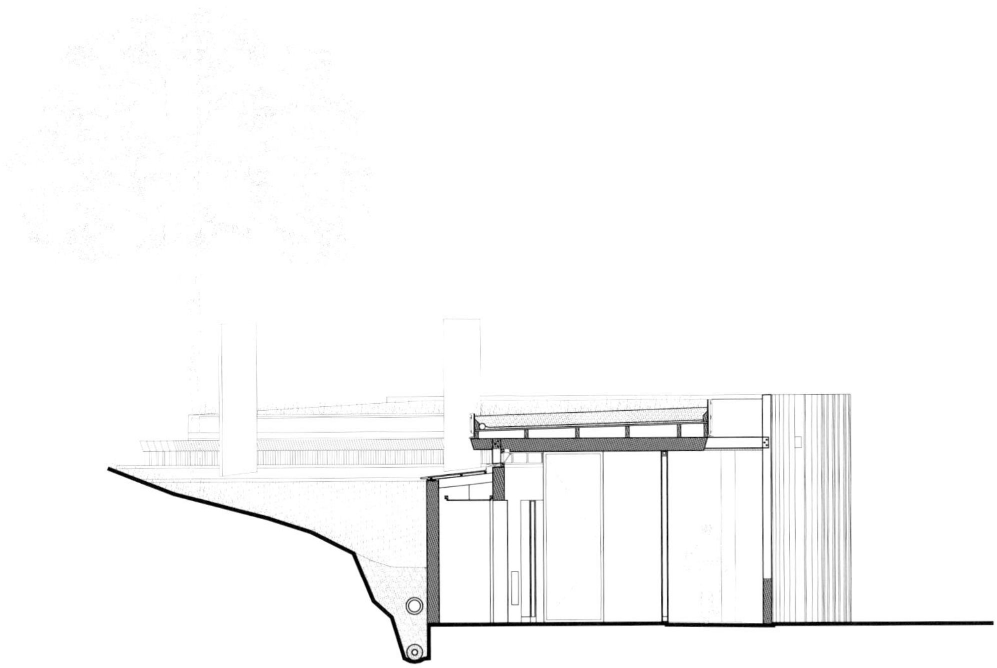

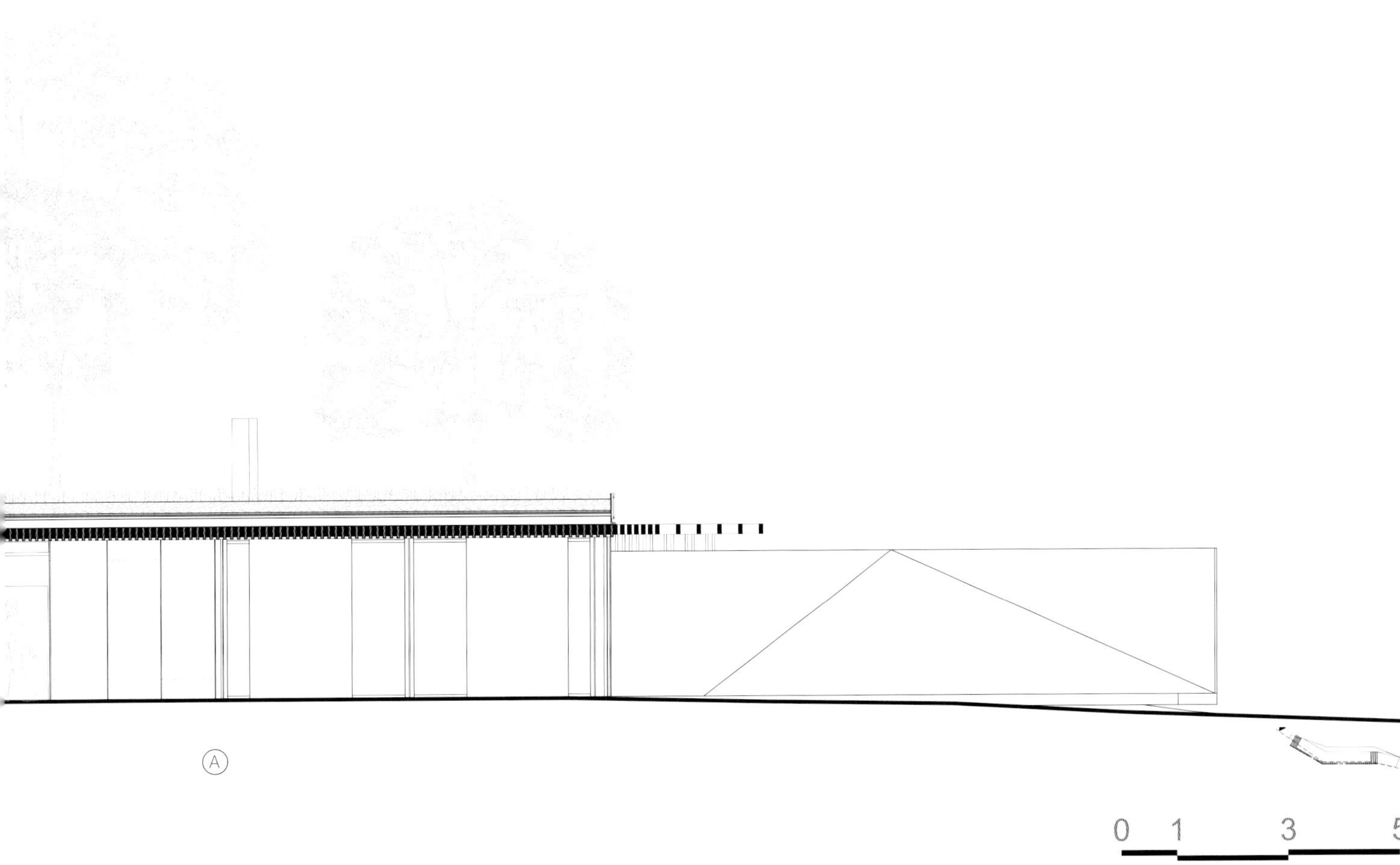
A
0 1 3 5

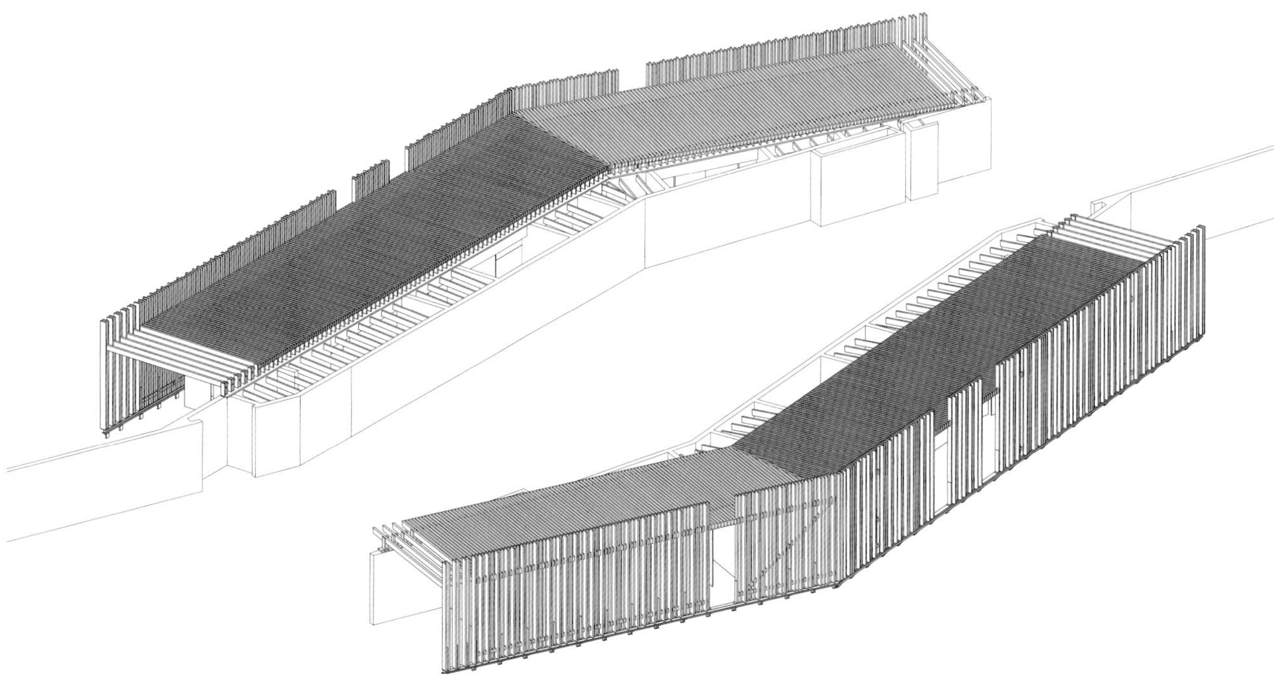

Technical detail

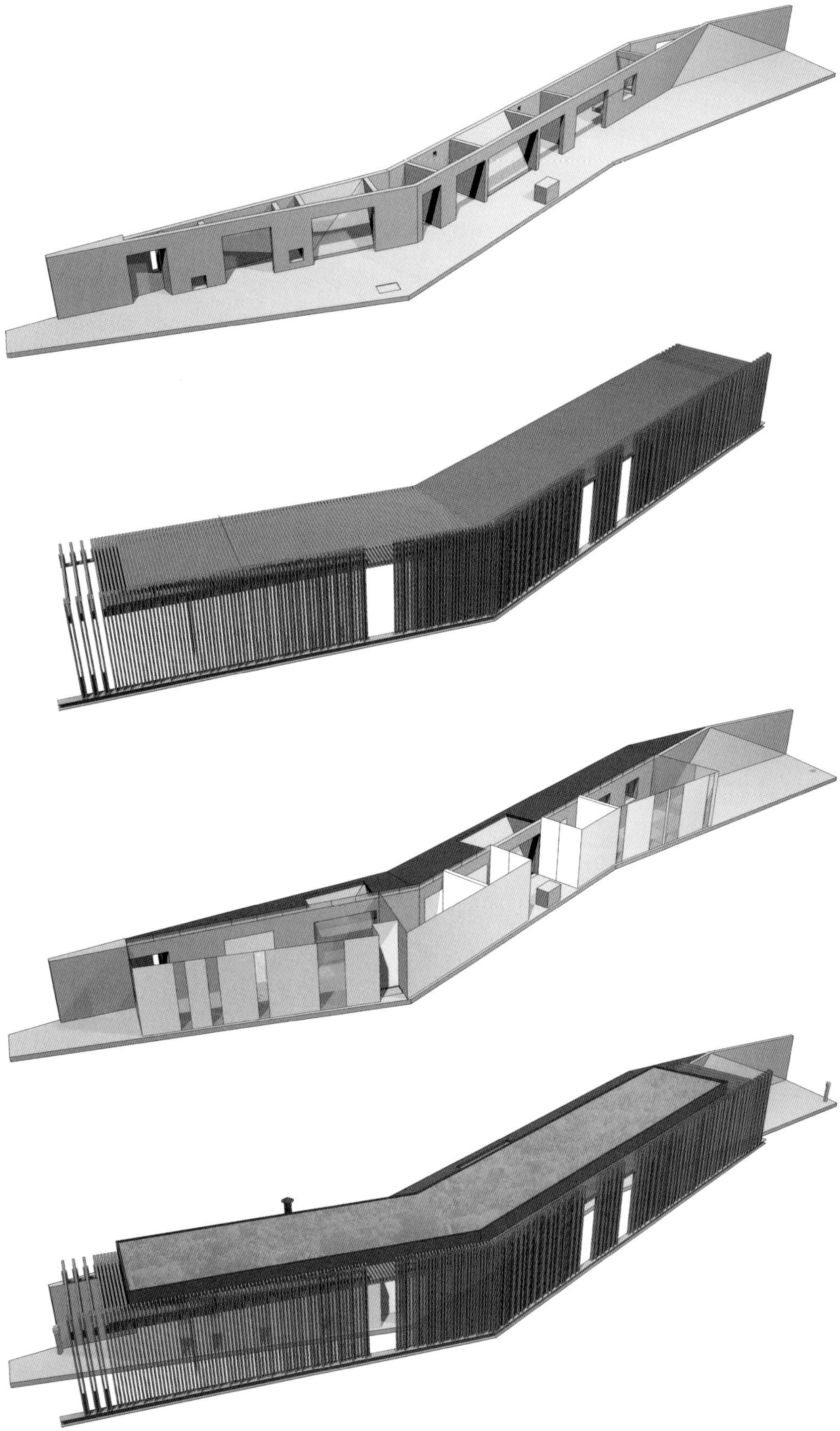

Exploded axonometric

Construction

MANITOU

The Building

Can Gio Pavilion

Description

Project Credits

Firm Location
HCMC Vietnam

Completion Year
2020

Gross Built Area
350 m²

Project Location
Can Gio, Ho Chi Minh City, Vietnam

Photo Credits
Giuseppe De Fransco, Hiroyuki Oki

Design Team
Domitille Perrault, Tuyen Tran Minh, Pham Linh Da

Clients
La Maison de Can Gio

Landscape
DE-SO Asia Martin Jallais

Structural and M&E Engineers
RFR VN

Pavilion Hangrove

| DE-SO ASIA, Olivier Souquet

Can Gio forest stretches over 75,740 ha land, which gather about 150 plant species.

Close to Ho Chi Minh City (60 km), this area is also considered as the green lung of the city with its typical mangroves possessing a variety of unique and rare species.

A bird wings-shaped building
Can Gio Restaurant is designed like a pair of bird wings spreading across the Can Gio Mangrove Forest located in the South of Ho Chi Minh City (the natural space was classified as one of the International Biosphere Reserves by UNESCO in 2000).

The wings forming a V shape frame up the view to the far horizon where the sun rises.

A natural mineral stone platform leveling up the base emphasizes this clear angle of view towards the mangrove horizon and the view to the appealing circular green lake in the front. The project is located in a touristic and populated area.

The project is designed as an opened public space, protected from the typical sunlight and heavy rains of the region by two V-shaped roofs. These large roofs function as a picture frame capturing all the beautiful surrounding landscape.

This sophisticated design adapts perfectly to the program desired by the Investor. The purpose is to create a welcoming area to receive visitors and a multi-functional space to organize various kinds of events: Conference and seminar meetings, temporary restaurant equipped with professional kitchen facilities, event functions for large groups and seasonal exhibitions.

The main facilities of the venue are:
- Two dining rooms equipped with air conditioning.
- A large kitchen with storage and chilled room.
- Sanitary areas.

This model complements the tourist planning which usually consisted of just hotels, resorts equipped with swimming pools, townhouses and villas, to offer an opportunity to go relaxing out of Ho Chi Minh city on the weekends.

The project must be able to cope with:
- The strong sun that whitens everything around
- Heavy rains and thunderstorms coming from the East Sea
- The dry wind

The color of the project is inspired by typical local sand color and mangrove trees roots.

The project also uses a light gray color similar to the silt which highlights the saturated green vegetation of the mangrove.

The roofs
The metal roofs (lozenge) resemble a pair of bird wings soaring up on the lagoon and sheltering the terraces.

These metal-framed roofs are covered on the underside with a folded and perforated metal sheet which lets light filtering inside. At night, the light coming from everywhere decorates these perforated metal (25%) mesh ceiling.

The base
The project used monolithic laterite stones to build the base in order to lift up the ground floor level and establish an architectural order so as to anchor the house into the sandy and silty site.

Ramps and stairs lead the way up to the terrace.

A central tree with ethereal foliage (Termilia Mantaly) brings shade and freshness to the terrace.

The four pentagonal buildings are made of concrete and covered with gray laterite stone. They are unitary.

This laterite is also used in massive stones of 10cm thickness to create the lattice wall for closed and air-conditioned dining rooms.

At night the lattice plays as a Vietnamese lantern diffusing the saturated color on the walls of the interior spaces.

A particular site

The very strong sea winds at Can Gio (typhoons) have been taken into account in the dimensioning of the cantilever beam.

In the hot season the air is suffocating, hence there is a necessity to create shade and freshness. Indeed, the presence of the round lake of water and the high-levelled base make it possible to capture any refreshing breezes.

The inertia of the thick mineral walls brings freshness to the closed rooms.

Construction

Constructing a building in a harsh tropical climate like the Can Gio region is a technical and ecological challenge; the pavilions are built with local Vietnamese materials and with the minimum of composite materials.

The construction elements are elements of small sizes assembled. Can Gio is a peninsula accessible by ferry; it is difficult to deliver materials by boat and deliveries are always limited to small quantities.

It's about being strong, durable, withstanding heavy rain, the hot vertical sun, and skillfully taking advantage of the chill wind coming from the East sea.

Garden

The construction materials used are matte, only the glazed elements and the black and green ceramic pots imported from Bin Duong bring reflections. (These recall Mekong jars storing water or Nuoc mam.) A garden composed of tamarins surrounds the project.

History of the project

The DE-SO agency was contacted in 2010 to complete a master plan thought by Mr. Phuoc Loc, to design different types of terraced houses and a resort on 52 hectares in Can Gio.

The owner built the townhouses with another architectural firm as well as a 14-room hotel with a bar and tennis court.

In 2016, investors Nguyen Thuy Duong and Luong Viet Han contacted Olivier Souquet again and took up the landscaping project with the DE-SO Asia agency. They discussed in 2017 the concept of creating a central space fulfilling several reception functions. (A first canvas building created in 2011 was blown away by the strong winds.)

In 2018 the agency studied the pavilions which were to be built in 2019 by the owner who himself directed the works, and the agency provided the owner guidelines for the landscape.

In 2021, the agency designed 29 luxury villas, a 60-room resort, and the reception houses of the resort which is opened towards the mangrove (including a restaurant, spa, and a complementary building for the swimming pool).

The large swimming pool of 600 m² was built in 2019 and filled with water.

The reception houses are expected to be constructed in a short time.

Materials
The harsh climate of Can Gio requires the use of robust natural materials.

The choice is to avoid to have superimposition of materials and layers, but to feel the material is important.

The base and foundations are made of concrete, and the pavilions are made of massive laterite brick. The metal structure and the large overhang were made of metal frame. The windows behind the stone moucharabiehs are made of aluminum and the entrance doors to the rooms are made of exotic hardwood. The roof covering initially in zinc is a clear lacquered metal tray.

The use of natural materials such as laterite skate and take on the color of the environment. Their color is not dazzling in the sun.

Drawings

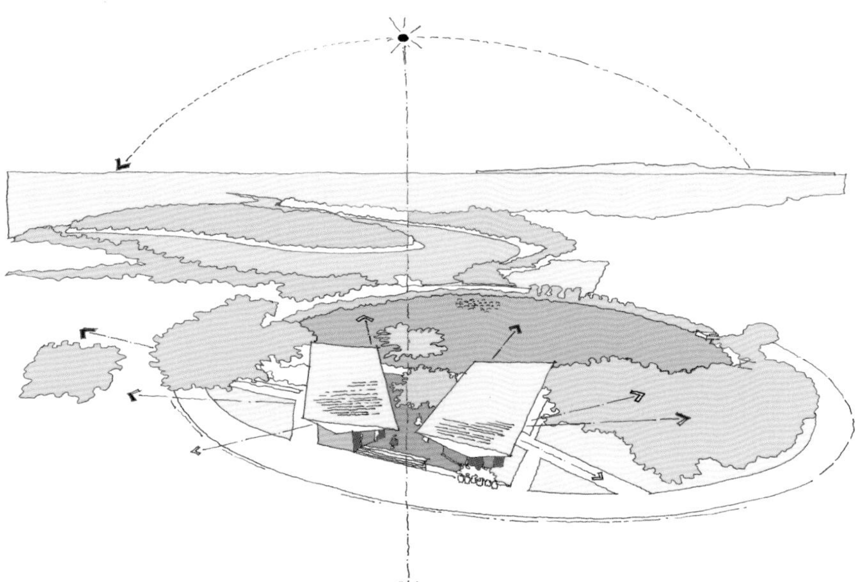

Sketch

Masterplan

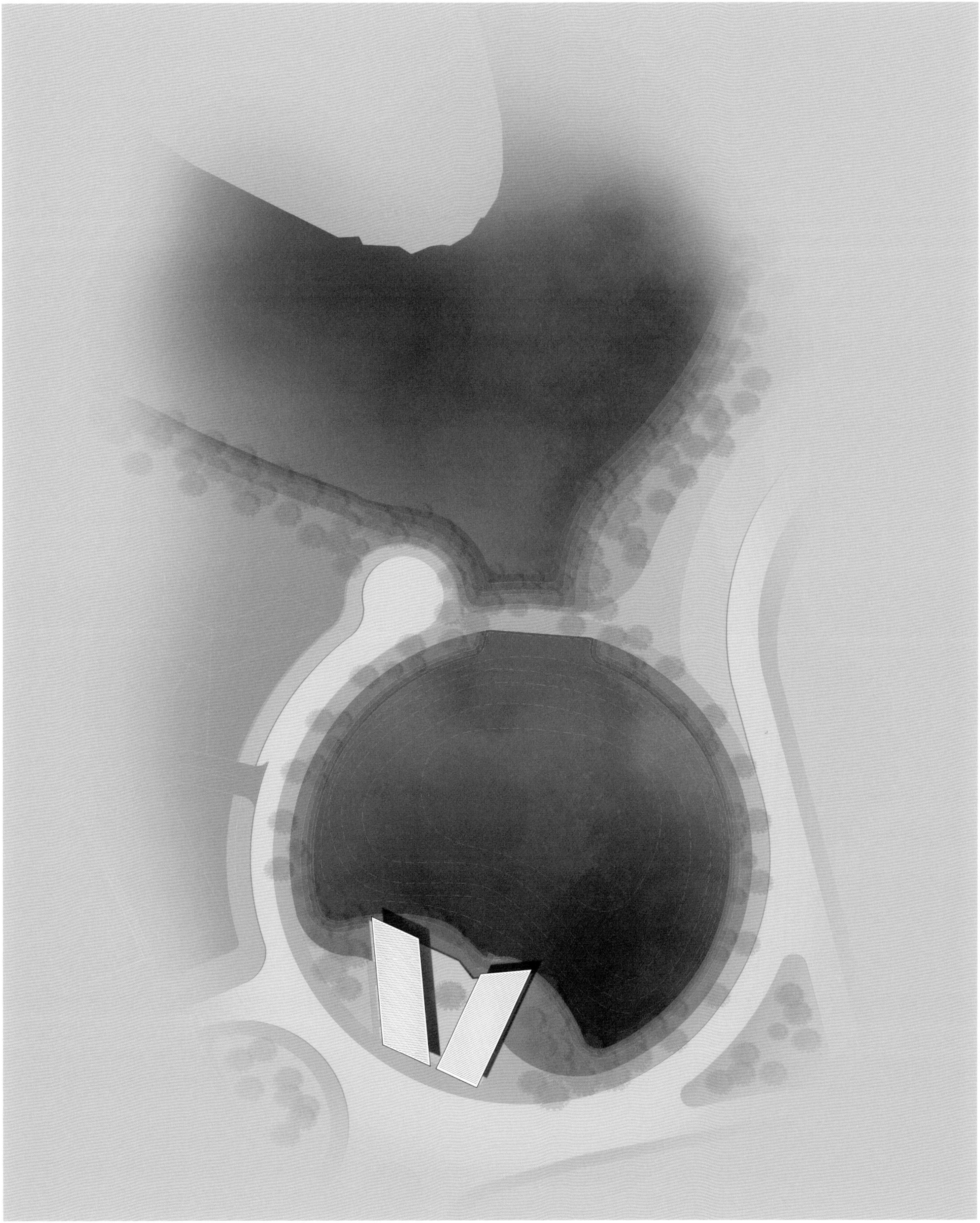

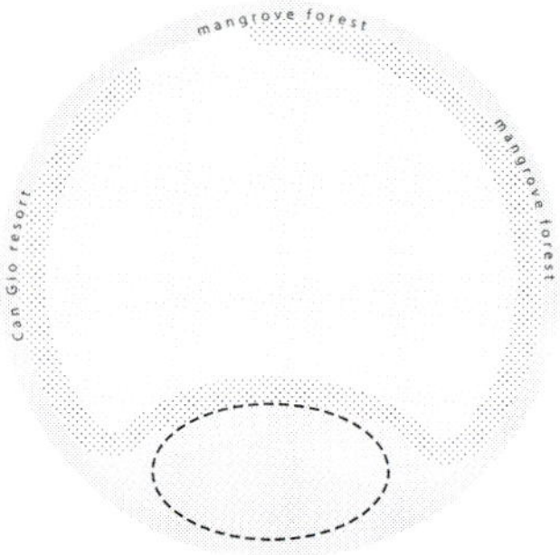

Project location

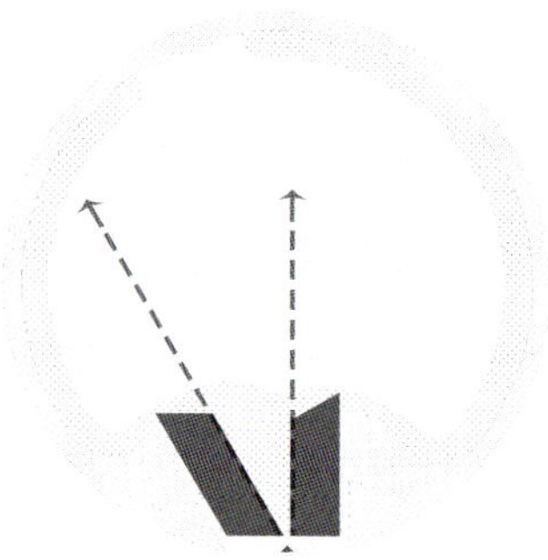

Capturing the surroundings

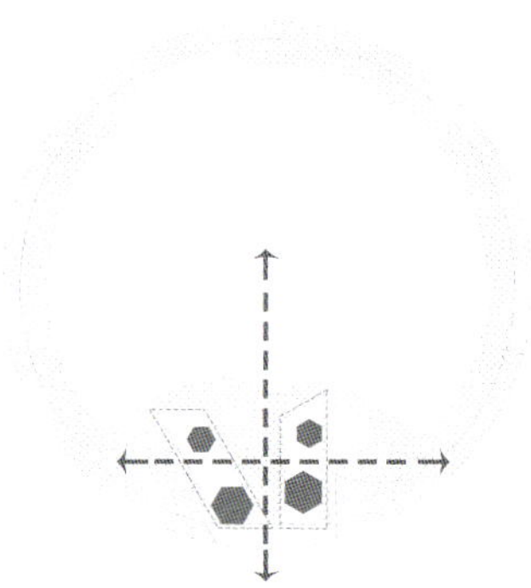

Voided volume-widened view

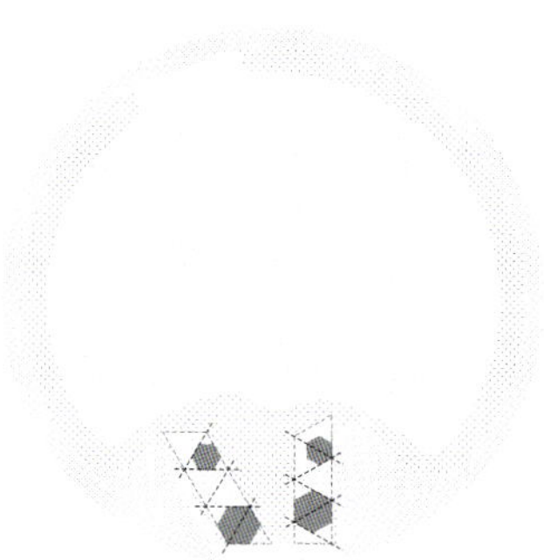

Geometry symmetry shape

Masterplan

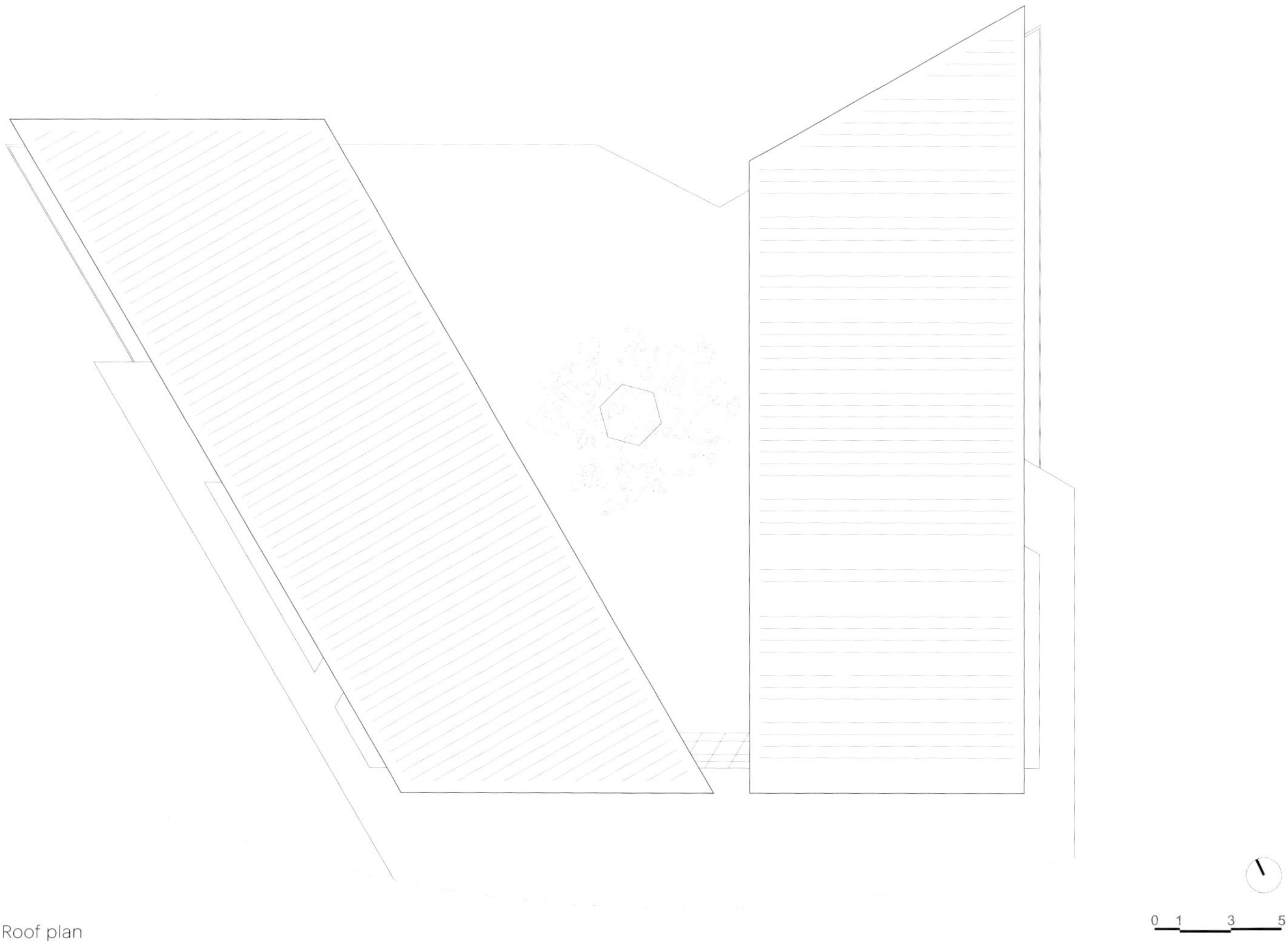

Roof plan

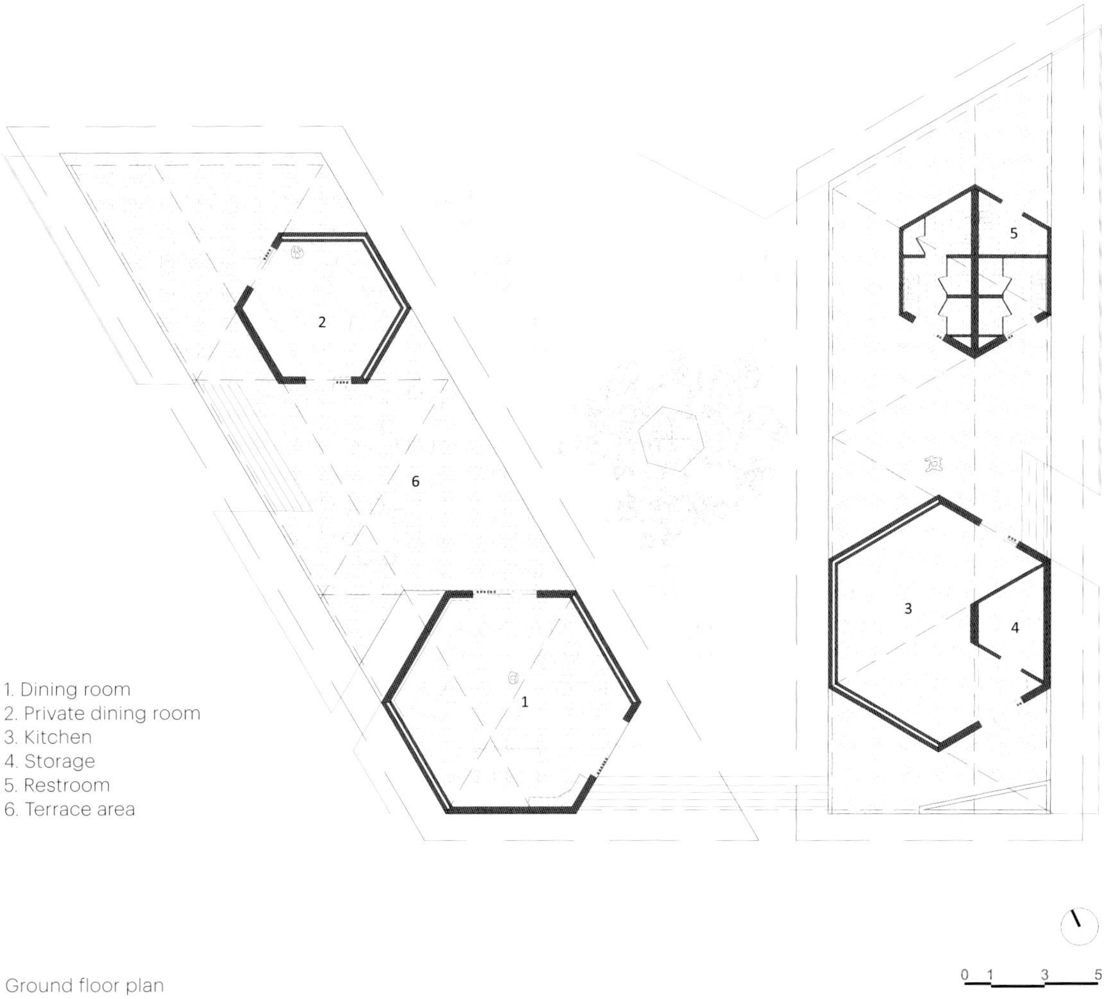

1. Dining room
2. Private dining room
3. Kitchen
4. Storage
5. Restroom
6. Terrace area

Ground floor plan

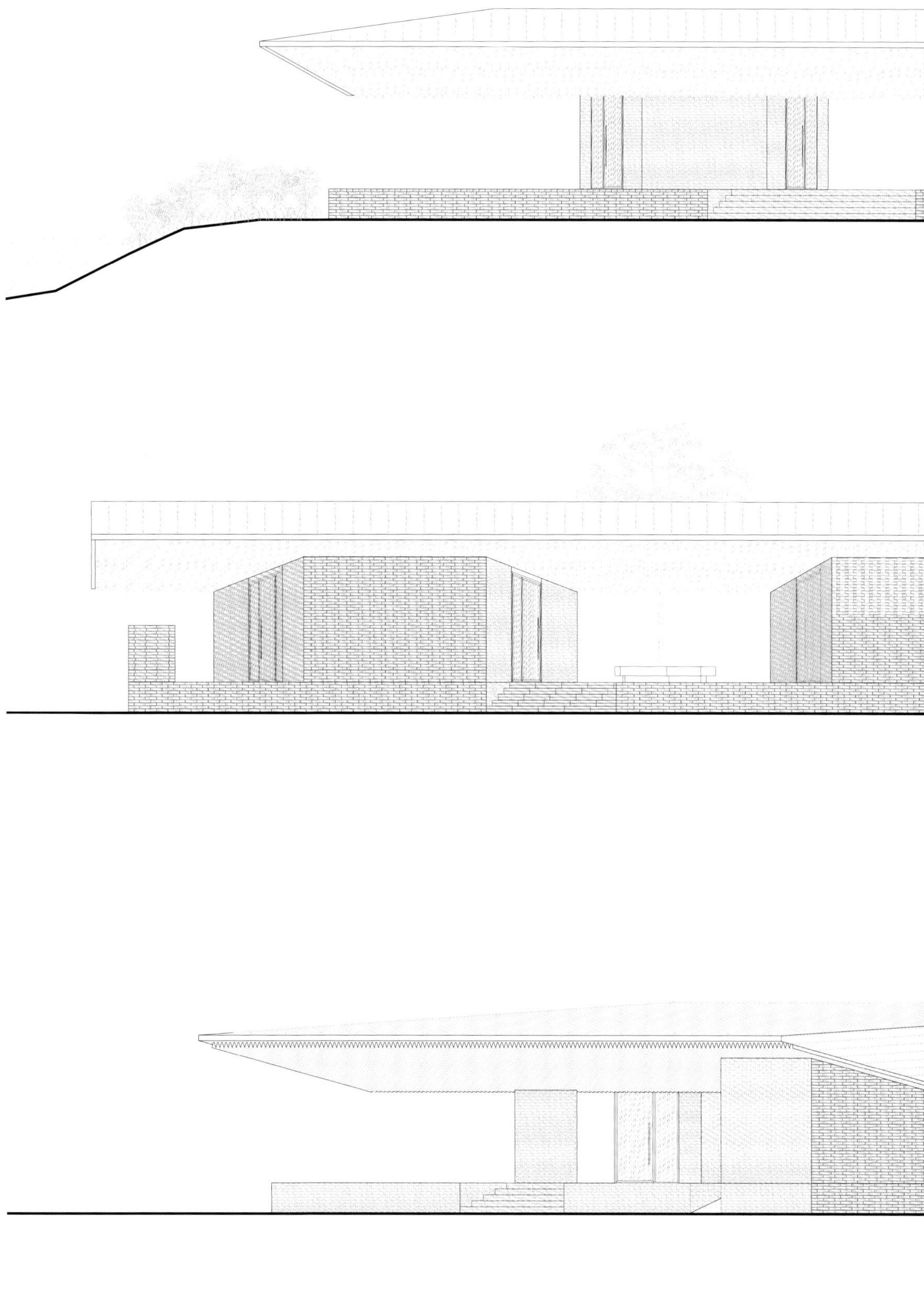

Elevations

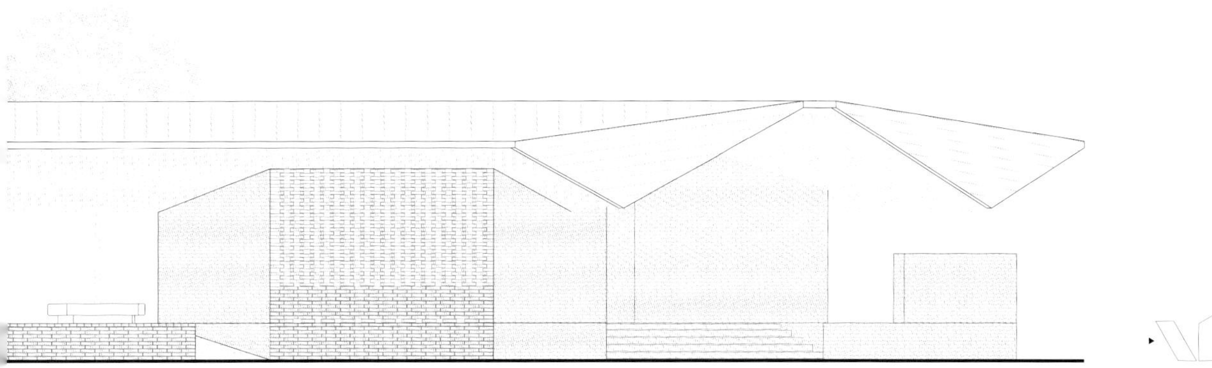

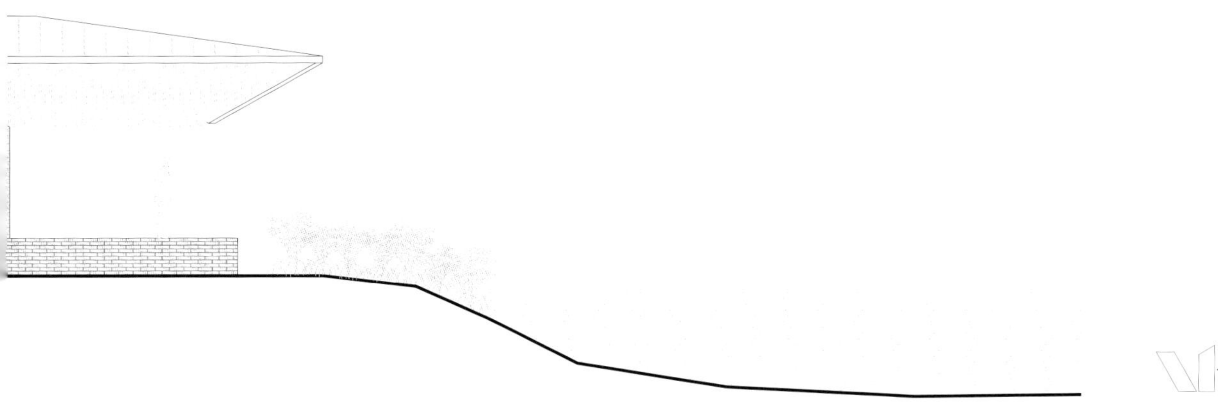

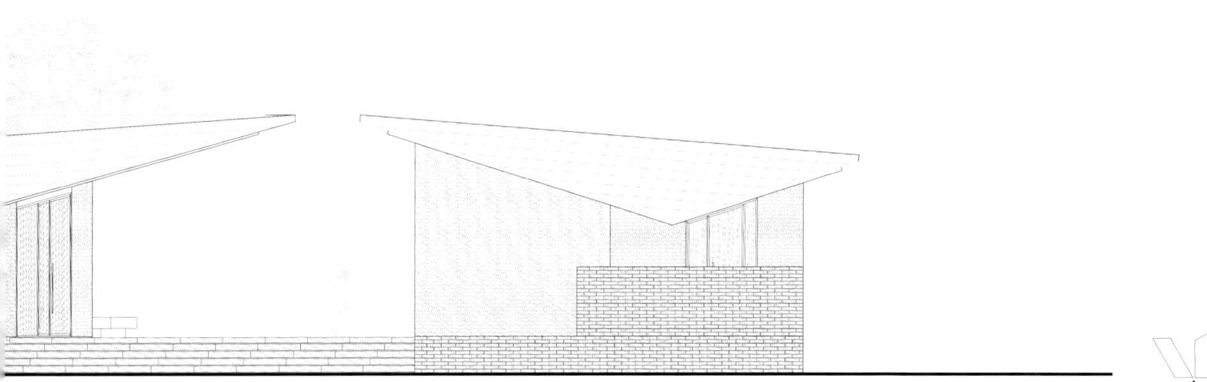

0 1 3 5

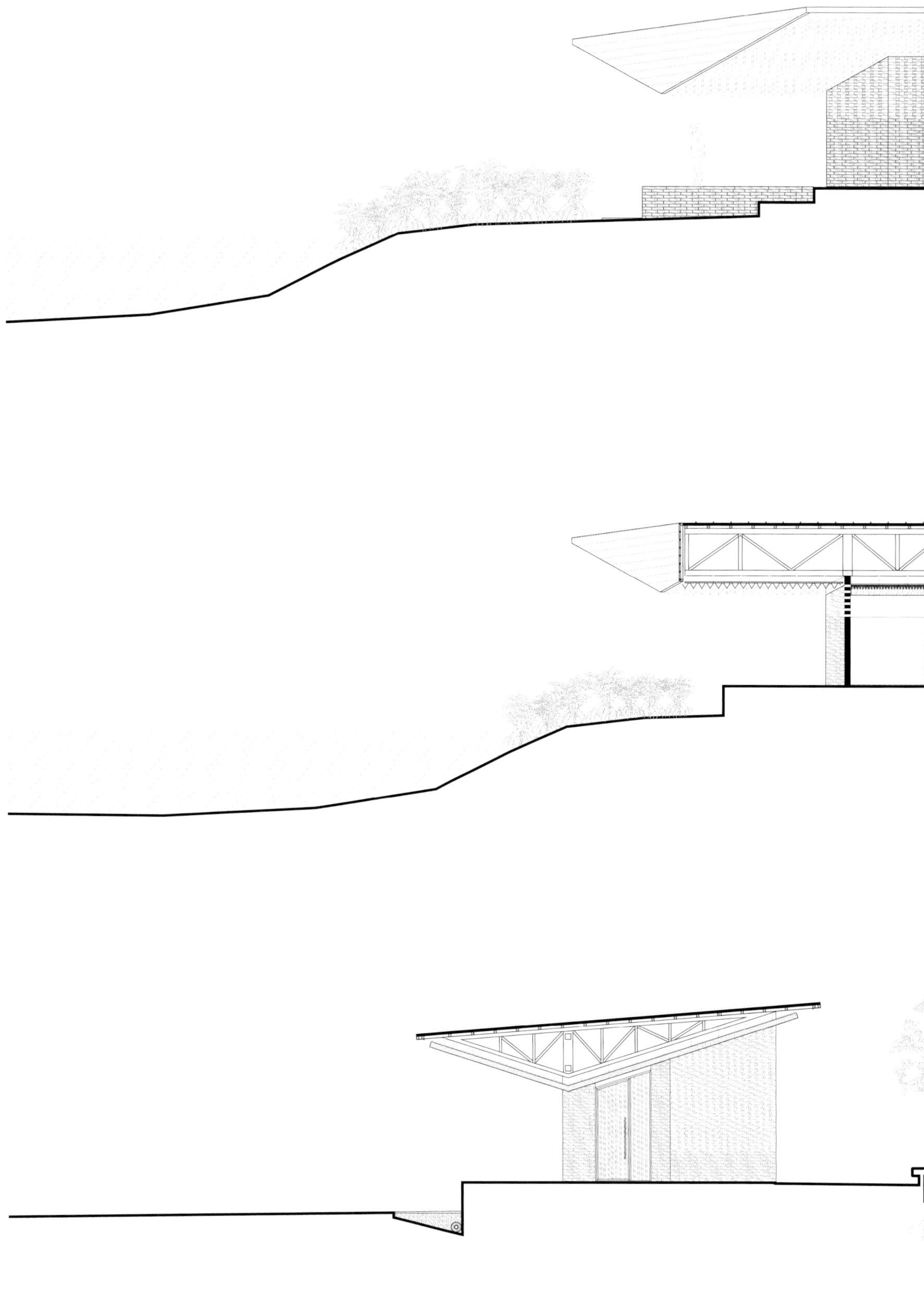

Sections

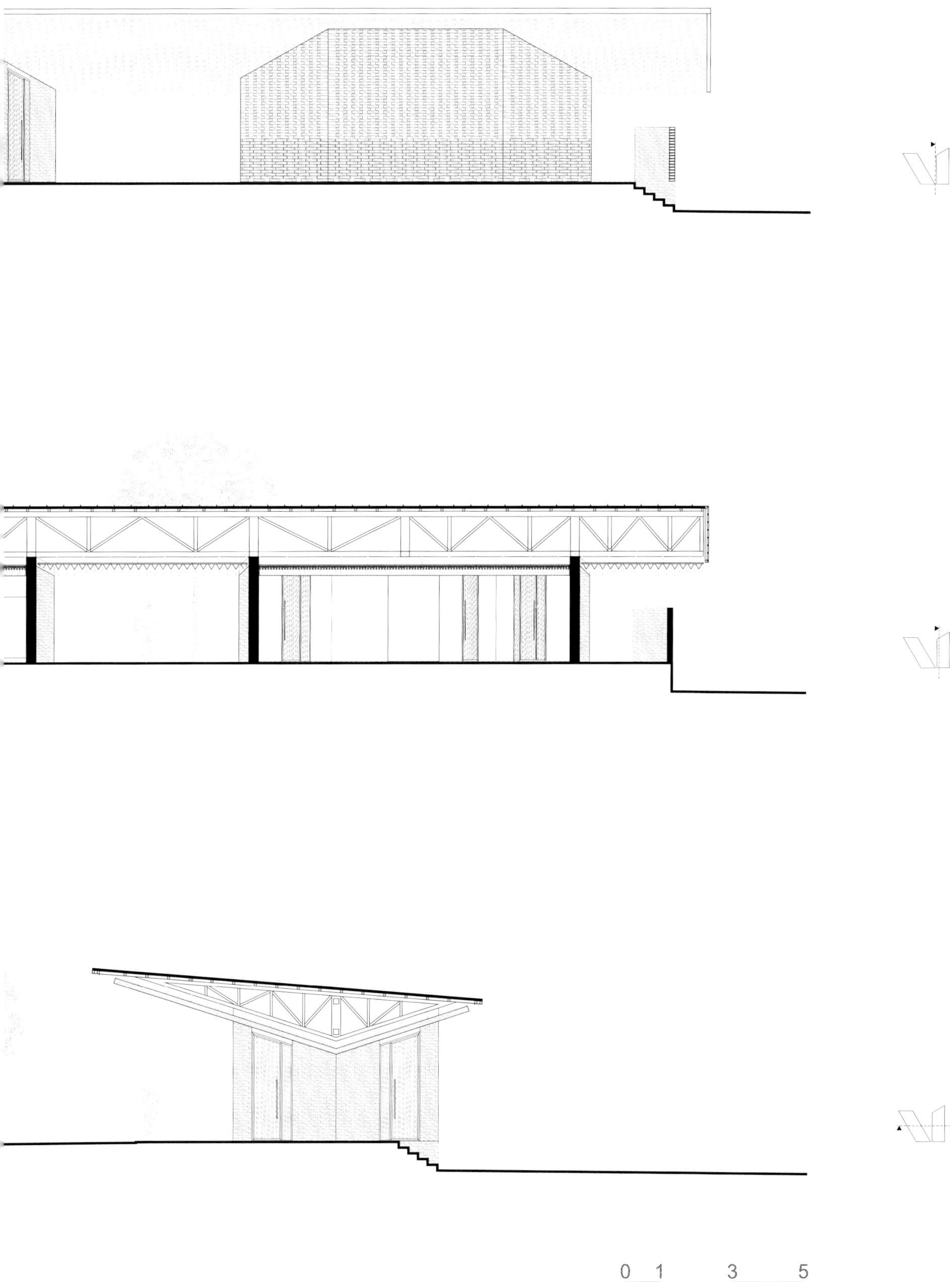
0 1 3 5

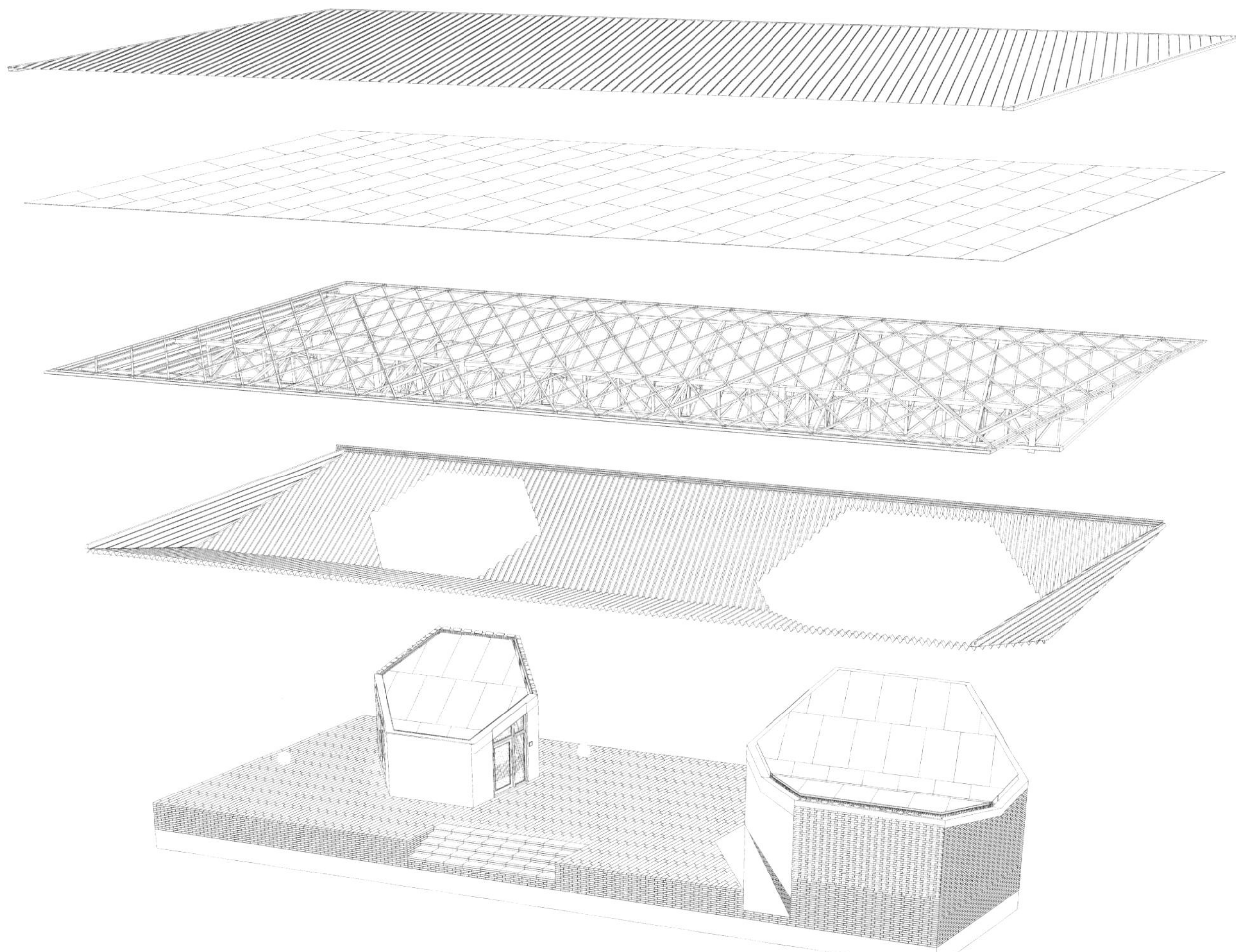

Restaurant frame structure

Roof structure layer
1. Aluminium roof
2. Wood plate
3. Steel purlin
4. Roof frame
5. Perforated ceiling 25% void
6. Wood louver ceiling

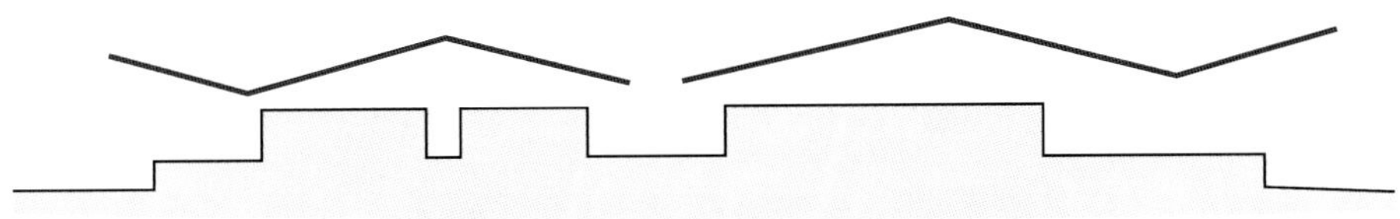

Grow from the soil-continuing material from ground to roof

Ventilation

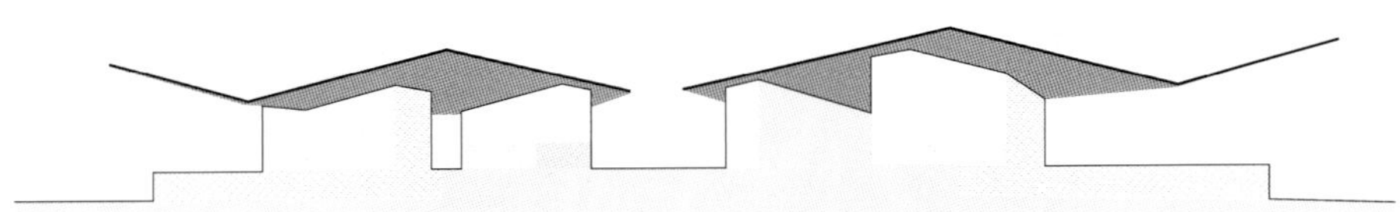

The outdoor terrace formed by functional enclosed blocks and above sloped perforated aluminium surface

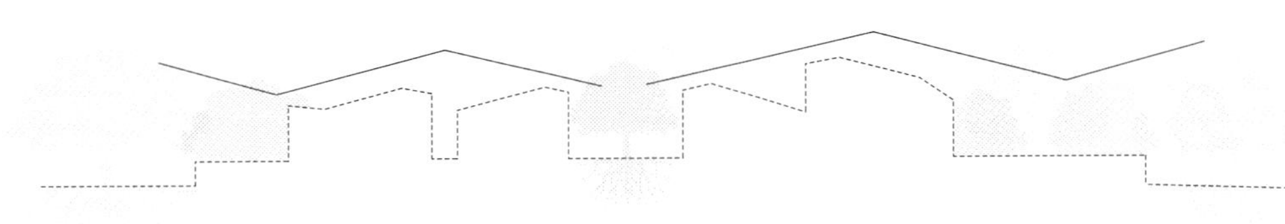

Capturing the view

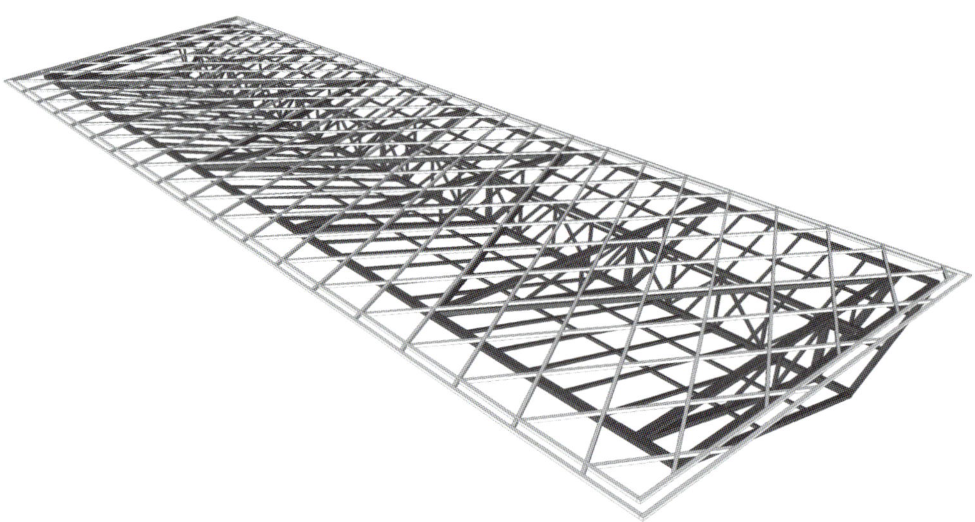

Construction

FILA

The Building

RESIDENCE & RESORT

Epilogue

Christine Dalnoky
Provence – March 2021

From the Bruoux mines in Provence, where I live, yellow ochres have been extracted that, for past centuries, colored the façades of Saigon, where Olivier Souquet lives.

As a metaphor for the history of ochre, today a tourist attraction where we initially worked together, these mines are at the origin of a series of projects where architecture is indelibly interwoven into nature and the landscape.

The landscape relates the history – histories – that our projects recall and perpetrate.

The Bruoux project reminds us to what extent the site itself is the project, since initially hewn by the miner tools.

The mine now closed, we simply direct visitor attention and the itinerary – between the forest and the spectacular rock face to access the ochre galleries to make them aware of the work accomplished and pay the miners tribute.

In the foreground, the vertical tree trunk façade of the reception building is punctuated by light and shadow, as in the sunlit forests of Provence. Far from being an architectural statement, it is both a passage and a shelter where the interior and exterior, shadow and light, mingle like a filter that prepares us for the delightful discovery of the ochre cliff face.

Still a few ochre seams, a few ledges on which to sit and contemplate, suffice.

In Can Gio, protection from violent typhoons and, on occasions, the stifling heat are necessary.

The gentle lake landscape is contemplative.

The architecture shelters – protects from the wind, frames the views, filtres light and encourages contemplation… without anything unnecessary or superfluous. The pavilions enable us to appreciate the climate, to see the landscape in their full meaning.

The two projects can be considered as prototypes of a way to think about the city through landscape.

They seek to re-establish a serene relationship between a site and its natural habitat, however small the project may be.

By articulating the geometry between history and people, and its geography, to enhance its uniqueness – the identity of place – quite simply.

Quite naturally, the ecological question is resolved at this intersection of the two eras – years, even centuries of history and its geographical age.

Rather than a spatial, the project works with time – the timeline is people!

The art of the essential to open up the field of possibilities, an essential renaissance that brings about intelligent and lasting change.

Christine Dalnoky, born in 1956, is a French landscape architect and educator. She graduated from the ENSP, Versailles, in 1982. In 1988, she founded her own office with Michel Desvigne. Among her works: Port Marianne Area, Montpellier; the TGV train stations in Valence, Avignon and Marseilles; Sieroterapico Park, Milan; Millennium Park, London; Middelheim Museum, Antwerp; Museum of Modern Art, Kirchberg. She has lectured at the ENSP in Versailles, Genoa Institute of Architecture and the Architecture Academy in Mendrisio.

Appendix

DE-SO
François DEFRAIN and Olivier SOUQUET

After a decade of collaboration, François Defrain and Olivier Souquet co-founded DE-SO Architecture agency in 1995 in Paris and together they have gradually affirmed their position via many international awards and achievements. These accomplishments have demonstrated the highly-demanding quality and innovative thinking in DE-SO's approach to architecture and design.

The agency has 4 shareholders and more than 30 associates who have carried out many public, cultural and educational projects, alongside with other residential and urban planning ones. One of the most remarkable strengths of the agency is its emphasis on public architecture (libraries, theaters, music conservatories, and schools) and cultural architecture (museums, heritage sites, etc.).

In France, DE-SO has been working with Louis Vuitton since 2019 to design their production workshops for leather and bags in different regions of France.

The agency creates guiding plans for large territories, and undertakes coordination missions, town planning projects and enhancements of remarkable sites.

As part of our commitment to exporting our outlook and expertise, especially in Southeast Asia, in 2016 DE-SO have opened a Vietnamese office in Hô Chi Minh City, DE-SO Asia.

Each project's intended uses, functionality and materials are all underpinned by our mastery of the drawing, where geometry meets geography.

DE-SO Asia. Vietnam, HCMC.

Expertise in Public and Culture Architecture & Urban Planning
In Vietnam, DE-SO keeps imposing the predominant strength in public and culture architecture and on urban planning throughout many successful projects. Gaining significant reputation in the industry, DE-SO Asia has collaborated with various private investors and public developers such as the Departments of Construction in different cities to develop complex urban planning areas, from small to large scales of both rural and urban zones across the country. To name a few, the *Thu Thiem New Urban Area Construction Project*, a strategic development of the City in the beginning of the 21st century developed by Ho Chi Minh City People's Council; *Thi Nai Lagoon* developed by the DOC of Binh Dinh; *President Hô Chí Minh Memorial Special National Relic Site* in Nam Dan, Nghe An as part of the national plan to foster culture-history tourism in Vietnam & *Ham Rong Nui Do Area in Thanh Hoa*, both developed by T&T Group.

Moreover, thanks to a wide network of local and international partners, a strong connection of multicultural professional workers in Vietnam and France, DE-SO has the ability to offer a complete professional service package in varying industries to cater the needs of a wider range of customers in an emerging market such as hospitality, residential housings, hospitals, heritage sites, etc.

Notable architecture & landscape projects: *City Planning Exhibition Center of Ho Chi Minh City* on Thu Thiem Peninsula; *Van Hien University* of Hung Hau Group, *Hausnima residences* of EZLand, *Resort and ecological villas at the mangrove biosphere reserve of Can Gio* of Phuoc Loc company.

Creating a unique identity and a harmonious environment
Our identity relies on our in-depth expertise in the locality features of different regional areas combined with the "savoir faire" to apprehend and incorporate sophisticatedly these features into our designs and planning works.

DE-SO. France, Paris.

Our designs dedicate a special attention attributed to the surrounding environment of each project. The harmonious integration of local practices, cultural functions and local materials is directly shown on each drawing, through which the relationship between geography and geometry is resolved in the finest and most optimal way.

Our environmental concern in a broad sense is indicated in sustainable construction, optimization of costs and materials, prioritization of organic materials. In the context of multiple ecological changes happening on a global scale, research on innovation and use of sustainable materials such as the use of wood is playing a challenging yet essential role in our mission's approach.

Together with a dynamic team of 20 people in Vietnam, DE-SO Asia is willing to keep moving forward, to constantly innovate and expand our fields of expertise in order to bring diversified services which are of highest quality standards to our clients in Asia and worldwide.

"L'architecture est un art de l'assemblage.
Il s'agit d'ancrer dans un site un projet.
Allier finement géographie et géométrie, en révélant le génie du lieu.
Composer des fenêtres sur le paysage et les multiples horizons qui existent."

"Architecture is an art of assemblage.
It is about anchoring a project in a site.
Finely combining geography and geometry, revealing the genius loci.
To compose windows on the landscape and the multiple horizons that exist."

Olivier Souquet

Louis Vuitton Factory

2021-2019
St-Pourçain-sur-Sioule (03)
Size: 7.454 m² gfa

Youth cutural center

2021-2019
HCMC, Vietnam
Size: 16.000 m² gfa

Van Hien University

2021-2019
HCMC, Vietnam
Size: 16.000 m² gfa

Ho Chi Minh Special Memorial Area

2022-2018
Nghe An, Vietnam
Size: 287ha project area
Invited Competition - First Prize, 2018
1/500 planning, 2020

Refurbishment and Elevation of the EPA-Orsa Headquarter

2014-2010
Choisy-le-Roi (94)
Size: 1.668 m²
Cost: 3,2 M €

Multipurpose Complex

2014-2010
Mazan (84)
Size: 1.850 m²
Cost: 3,5 M €
1st prize fibra award 2019
1st national winner Bois 2013 Public Building

Ho Chi Minh City Planning Exhibition Center

2022-2011
HCMC, Vietnam
Size: 18.000 m² gfa
Cost: 20 M €

F. Dorléac School

2015-2011
Complex, 26 classrooms
Paris
Size: new 3.300 m² + refurb. 4.925 m²
Cost: 19,5 M €
Winner Trophées Bois 2015

D. Mitterrand School Complex 20 classrooms

2015-2011
Pierrefitte-Sur-Seine
Size : 4.600 m²
Cost: 9,2 M € (excl. taxes)

Music and Dance

2014-2011
Conservatory
Melun
Size: 3.170 m²
Cost: 7,3 M €

Refurbishment and Expansion of Lycée R. Doisneau

2018-2009
Corbeil-Essonnes (91)
Size: 27.730 m²
Cost: 27 M €

Cultural Center Media Library & Music Conservatory

2014-2009
Evry (91)
Size: 2.375 m²
Cost: 7,6 M €

Thu Thiem Central Plaza and Riverside Park

2022-2008
HCMC, Vietnam
Size: 25ha
Cost: 73 M €

Cultural Complex

2009-2007
Alfortville
Size: 4.544 m²
Cost: 9,9 M €

Expansion of the Grenoble Water Station (38)
2005-2007
Grenoble
Size: 180 m²
Cost: 0,37 M €

Book Credits

Art Direction: Oscar Riera Ojeda
Graphic Design: Lucía B. Bauzá
French to English Translation: Nicholas Harding
Copy-editing: Kit Maude & Michael W. Phillips Jr.

OSCAR RIERA OJEDA
PUBLISHERS

ISBN 978-1-946226-47-1

Published by Oscar Riera Ojeda Publishers Limited
Printed in China

Oscar Riera Ojeda Publishers Limited
Unit 1003-04, 10/F.,
Shanghai Industrial Investment Building,
48-62 Hennessy Road, Wanchai, Hong Kong
T: +852-5311-1625

Production Offices | China
Suit 19, Shenyun Road,
Nanshan District, Shenzhen 518055
T:+1-484-502-5400

www.oropublishers.com | www.oscarrieraojeda.com
oscar@oscarrieraojeda.com